HOPE FOR THE TROUBLED

Also by Lucy Freeman

FIGHT AGAINST FEARS

HOPE FOR THE TROUBLED

by

LUCY FREEMAN

CROWN PUBLISHERS, INC. :: NEW YORK

Copyright, 1953, by Lucy Freeman

Library of Congress Catalog Card Number: 53-5680

Printed in the United States of America
American Book–Stratford Press, Inc., New York

"Perfect Love casts out Prudery
together with Fear."

RICHARD GARNETT

Contents

To My Mother

Acknowledgment

My deepest thanks go to all who have, with patience and sympathy, given me help in my job as reporter, trying to bring to the public a deeper understanding of the art of healing the psychic wounds that keep many from happiness. Were I to list the names, it would take up all the pages of the book. Special gratitude goes to Dr. John C. Thurrott, psychoanalyst, whose wisdom and compassionate philosophy enabled me to gain some convictions of my own.

Deepest thanks of all go to my husband, Harry Becker, who, with courage and conviction, has spent his life working to improve the well-being of mankind. In spite of the arduous demands of his current assignment, finding ways and means to bring comprehensive hospital services within reach of all, he found time to help plan the book, make valuable suggestions and encourage me to write it.

Lucy Freeman

HOPE FOR THE TROUBLED

CHAPTER 1

The Touch of Trouble

A CHILD'S scream pierces the silent night.

His mother runs to the dark room, turns on the light. "What happened, dear?" she asks fearfully.

The child, eyes holding terror, stares at his mother as though she were a stranger.

"A big, black bear's after me," he says, starting to cry. "He wants to bite my head off."

Why has a dream become so threatening to a child?

[15]

A woman pulls the king of hearts from her hand, exposing the card to the other bridge players.

Her husband, sitting across from her, looks at her with open contempt.

She sees his expression, puts the card back.

"Play it—you started to!" her husband demands.

She does. When the hand is finished, the husband pushes his chair from the table angrily.

"How can you be so stupid as not to know I held the ace?" he asks. "Don't you *ever* learn anything? This is the last time I play bridge with you."

Why has the playing of a single card become so important?

*   *   *

A middle-aged man stands in a thickly carpeted Wall Street office, staring out the window. His partner walks into the room, carrying a sheet of paper.

"We doubled our net this past six months, thanks to that hunch of yours," says the partner.

The man at the window does not turn.

"What are you looking at?" the partner asks curiously.

"At the people down on the street," says the man who has just doubled his firm's income. He adds reflectively, "So unlike me. They seem to be going somewhere."

"Why do you say that?" asks his partner in surprise. "You can go any place, buy anything. You have a nice wife, good kids. What's missing?"

The man at the window hesitates, then says, "Happiness. I guess."

Why does a man who appears to have everything yearn for happiness?

*   *   *

A high-school girl rushes into the house, throws her school-books on the hall table, cries out, "Mother?"

"I'm up in the sewing room," calls down her mother.

The girl dashes upstairs. "Lydia asked me to go with her family to their farm this weekend. Isn't that wonderful?"

The mother stops sewing, looks at her daughter reprovingly. "You know I don't like Lydia or her friends. And her mother—"

In despair the girl breaks in, "But I told her I could go!"

"You'll have to call her up, then, and tell her you have other plans," the mother says flatly.

"But I can't. I won't!" The girl runs into her own room. She flings herself into a chair and hysterically screams, "How can she do this to me?"

Why should a mother's "no" cause such torment?

*   *   *

A husband lies in bed watching his wife put up her hair.

"Are you ever going to stop that?" he asks impatiently.

"Just a minute more, darling," she says.

He sighs. "I thought you wanted to go to bed early to-night."

Her mouth tightens. "I'm finished now." She drops the comb, clicks off the light.

He moves to touch her, then pulls away. He says tone-

[17]

lessly, "Let's sleep." He turns to the edge of the bed, anxious and tense.

"Good nig.t," she says. Her voice is controlled but her mouth quivers and her eyes start to fill with tears.

Why can't this husband and wife tell each other what they really want?

*　　*　　*

A teacher walks to a desk where a boy is staring at a map of South America in a geography book.

"Give me that note!" she orders.

"What note?" asks the boy, his eyes focussed even more intently on the map.

"I saw you trying to get Mary's attention by waving a note. Give it to me."

"I haven't got any note," says the boy, face paling.

She slaps him. He flushes, says nothing. She holds her head and shoulders high as she returns to the front of the room, breathing rapidly, blood rushing to her cheeks.

Why has this teacher reacted so violently to a schoolboy's note to his girl?

*　　*　　*

After the spasm of pain ends, a man picks up the telephone by the bed, calls his office.

"I won't be in today, Helen," he tells his secretary. "My damned ulcer has me down again. Sign those letters I dictated yesterday, cancel the trip to New York and call Bill in Dallas to meet me here tomorrow. If John's field memorandum isn't in today's mail, send him a wire to report here Friday."

As he hangs up, the doctor arrives. "The old ulcer, eh?" he asks breezily.

"Good God, doc," says the man, wincing. "The diet you gave me has made it worse."

The doctor examines him, then announces seriously, "We've got to get you to the hospital this time. You need some expert treatment—out of reach of telephone and office."

"I don't want to go to the hospital," says the man anxiously. "I don't have time. My business will go to pot. Isn't there something else we can do?"

"It's too late for anything else now," says the doctor. "As you know, we should have got at the cause of this earlier."

"Couldn't. Too busy," says the man.

He turns his face to the wall. He recalls that the doctor mentioned some connection between his intense need to work and the ulcer.

Why must a man drive himself so frantically that he falls ill?

* * *

These are among the troubled. Part of a silent army, they walk alone even in the largest crowd. They may escape for the moment into tavern, dance hall or theater, but when they come out into darkness, once again they face inescapable loneliness.

There is no one they can tell what they feel, no one who listens and understands. Their tears fall unseen, their words go unheard, their wishes unfulfilled.

[19]

It does not matter whether a man lives in Park Avenue penthouse or East Side slum. Trouble does not respect the dollar sign.

Nor whether he wears a Phi Beta Kappa key or has never opened a book. Trouble spares neither the educated nor uneducated.

And it does not matter whether he is ready for the tomb or just out of the womb. Trouble holds no reverence for years.

The troubled hold little faith in the future. They lack the vision that enables man to walk his way in wisdom and comfort.

"Where there is no vision, the people perish," warns the Bible.

The troubled feel themselves slowly perishing.

CHAPTER 2

"Who Love Too Much—"

"ALL the world is queer save thee and me, and even thou art a little queer."

Thus wrote Robert Owen upon breaking off business relations with his partner in 1828.

Some still hold this sentiment, believing everyone except themselves is troubled. Others feel that everyone including themselves is troubled. Still others say no one is really troubled—he only *thinks* he is.

Is there an answer to the question: Who are the troubled?

[21]

All of us have seen the same thing happen to different people with different results.

One man loses his job and, afraid to go home and tell his wife, heads for the nearest bar. A second man loses his job and immediately goes out to look for another.

One woman, hearing of the death of a friend, sinks into a depression, refusing to eat or see anyone. Another woman, in the same situation, accepts the fact that people die and, although grieving, goes about her daily routine.

One boy is punched in the eye by a classmate and feels so cowed he refuses to return to school. Another boy, who also receives a black eye, shows up in class that day, laughing at himself for not having ducked the blow.

One baby, scratched by a pin, screams as though his very life were threatened. Another baby, scratched by a pin, looks alarmed at first, then acts as though nothing out of the way had happened.

That a man is fired does not mean he is worthless. That a woman loses a friend through death does not mean she is wholly abandoned. That a boy was beaten in one fight does not mean he will lose all fights. That a pin scratches a baby does not mean he will die.

The untroubled take trouble in their stride. The troubled make of it torment. As Edmund Vance Cooke once wrote:

> Oh, a trouble's a ton, or a trouble's an ounce,
> Or a trouble is what you make it,
> And it isn't the fact that you're hurt that counts,
> But only how did you take it.

Trouble is a matter of degree. Some are relatively untroubled. Some are slightly troubled. Some are considerably troubled. Some are severely troubled. The relatively untroubled have an even temper, alert mind, pleasant disposition, understanding nature. They do not fret themselves unnecessarily, nor do they inflict their woes on the world. They appear happy to others.

What is happiness? It may be presumptuous to answer for more than oneself as to what happiness is, for each man has his dream of it.

"Do you have a happy life?" Ernest Hemingway was asked by Harvey Breit, of The New York Times Book Review section.

"I have never heard a happy life defined," replied Mr. Hemingway.

Many think of happiness as a goal, not a way of life. But rather than the pot of gold at the rainbow's end, happiness may be a steady flow of satisfaction that comes from within. It may not be made up of moments of high elation followed by deep despair but of a consistent feeling of peace and quiet pleasure.

Happiness flows out of feeling good about oneself. Cyril Connolly, the English writer, says: "We cannot be happy until we can love ourselves without egotism and our friends without tyranny."

If we love ourselves without egotism, we will love our friends without tyranny. For the urge to tyrannize stems from egotism.

Happiness does not necessarily free a man from practical

troubles. "Man is born unto trouble, as the sparks fly upward," the Bible tells us. But the way a man meets difficulties tells whether he is troubled or untroubled.

Both the happy and unhappy face the same problems—growing up, making friends, getting a job, marriage, children, and death of loved ones. When a man accepts all this as part of living, with confidence and trust in his decisions, he is untroubled. When each event in his life becomes a crisis, he is troubled.

The persistence of a certain pattern of life gives a clue to how troubled a man may be. One sneeze does not mean the grippe; nor a slight fever, pneumonia; nor a minor itch, a serious skin disease. But sneeze after sneeze, fever after fever and itch after itch indicate something is astir.

The man out of a job for the first time because his firm has collapsed or because he decides to give up accounting and study architecture is not necessarily troubled. But the one always out of a job, who can never find a satisfactory employer and who blames the world for unemployment, is troubled.

Nature meant us to be temperate, to possess everything in moderation. When we become excessive in deed, thought or emotion, nature is signalling us we are troubled. An "over" or "under" quality bespeaks suffering.

Those who overeat and those who starve; those who drink too much and those who dare not touch a drop; those who sleep endlessly and those who cannot sleep, are among the troubled.

As are those who laugh too much and those who cannot laugh; those whose tears spill freely and those who cannot cry; those who feel too deeply and those who feel little.

And those who have many and varied sexual experiences and those who have none; those who talk too much and those who are always silent; those who spend extravagantly and those who cannot spend.

Those with too much discipline and those without discipline; those who are aggressive and those who are submissive; those who are daring and those who are cautious; those who make a fetish of independence and those who are overly dependent; those who always want to be alone and those who cannot bear to be alone.

And those who are too clean and those who are too dirty; those who must have all things in order and those who must be disorderly; those who are too selfish and those who are too unselfish; those who rush through life as though it were a race, and those who cannot set forth to meet life.

As Alexander Pope wrote:

> Who love too much, hate in the like extreme;
> And both the golden mean alike condemn.

Pope meant by "love" the wild, hungry feeling that popularly passes for love, but which holds violence and fury. Real love is gentle, tender and enduring.

The untroubled live according to the golden mean and can, therefore, observe the Golden Rule. Those who dwell at either extreme of the golden mean are too troubled to observe any rules except the ones they create for themselves.

The middle path does not imply mediocrity. Those who live in ease are able to give all that is in them when the moment demands it. To meet emergencies they use the reserves built up out of happiness. The troubled display uncontrolled bursts of frenzy as they struggle blindly against the whole of life.

Some flaunt their troubled feelings; others hide them. There are those who insist they are not troubled although their lives reveal their unhappiness to others. Some do not know they are troubled; others freely admit their misery.

"My own outward appearance—ideally happy marriage, wonderful little girl, economic security—all give lie to my desperation underneath, and I wonder how many more there are like me, who to all who cannot see, appear normal as that ol' blueberry pie?" says one man who knows he is troubled.

And a woman who knows confesses, "In spite of all I have —a fine house, a handsome husband and two husky sons—a hidden terror often twists my stomach into knots and makes my head throb."

Some cannot bear the intensity of their troubled feelings and must destroy themselves to escape a world in which the pain is unendurable. It is as though inside them the spirits of terrorized children cried out to be released.

In their desperation, they may kill other men or themselves. Or they may build a fantastic, unreal world to which they retreat, living apart from all others.

But most of the troubled are not this desperate. They endure their despair, trapped but not knowing how to get free. They live, but it is in defiance of life, not enjoyment. They feel they are doomed to suffer—they do not know why.

CHAPTER 3

Fear—The Expert Marksman

Suffering does not spring full-blown from the spirit. Something causes it.

Why is it that one man can ride out a crisis, while the next collapses under it? Why is one man able to live in calm while another explodes in anger at the most picayune provocation?

What is it the untroubled possess which the troubled lack?

The untroubled man has faith in himself, loves himself.

"Love thy neighbor as thy self."

As thy self, the Bible says. Not instead of self, or in spite of self or for self.

If you love yourself, you will love others, be productive, lead a socially useful life, be mature—possess all those characteristics which describe the happy person.

If you do not love yourself, you cannot love anyone else. You radiate to the world the way you feel about yourself. Loving self is not selfish, because it leads to love of others, whereas without love of self, you only hate. When you hate someone else, you are really expressing hatred of yourself.

Instead of loving his neighbor as himself, the troubled person seems to hate his neighbor as himself. He feels as one man put it in describing a particular psychologist:

"He's a specialist in why people hate—for reasons other than that most people are hateful!"

Real love of self does not make you smug or conceited, but sympathetic and understanding. You accept yourself with all your faults and limitations. You give up the idea of being perfect, which no man can possibly be, a goal sought desperately only by those who are troubled. By accepting the imperfect self, you accept imperfections in others and in the world around you.

This does not mean passive resignation to injustice. But it rules out savage and self-hating perfectionism.

Why do the troubled hate themselves so intensely? Because they live in fear. Hate is the way they fight fear. Hate is the weapon nature gave us to save ourselves when we felt our lives threatened. The troubled person hates in order to save his life.

The untroubled do not fear except when their lives are actually at stake. The troubled always feel their lives in danger, not from real threats but from terrors inside themselves. They are constantly mobilized in hate to ward off these imaginary dangers.

A moderate amount of fear belongs to all, that we may act if our lives are in peril. If an invader points a gun at us we must feel fear, then hatred, to save our lives. But the troubled feel that when someone points a finger at them it is a gun. Fear causes anxiety, that nervous sensation which upsets minds and bodies. Anxiety may be a tightness in the stomach, a headache, a tenseness even unto brushing the teeth.

Fear may destroy a man, as in the legend of the pilgrim and the Plague.

Meeting the Plague, the pilgrim asked, "Where are you going?"

"I am going to Baghdad to kill 5,000 people," replied the Plague.

They met again a few days later. The pilgrim said to the Plague accusingly, "You killed 50,000 people instead of 5,000."

"No," said the Plague. "I killed only 5,000. The others died of fear."

Fear is a marksman that seldom misses. When fear strikes a man, he is lost unless somehow he gains new strength to cast fear off.

Fear is twice-vicious, for it may conceal itself, wearing disguises. It may keep a man from knowing he is afraid. Knowledge that he lives in fear may terrorize him far more than pretending he is not afraid.

Fear distorts reality; it is a microscope that blows up tiny shadows into monstrous shapes. Fear leaves small space for peace. James Norman Hall, the author, wrote:

> The thing that numbs the heart is this:
> That men cannot devise
> Some scheme of life to banish fear
> That lurks in most men's eyes.

Why does the troubled person live in fear? Because fear is what he has known all his life. He is conditioned to fear. As a child he grew up in an atmosphere of fear. Fear is familiar.

He feels like the boy taken to a doctor when he complained of severe stomach pains every morning.

"What do you do each morning?" asked the doctor.

"I get out of bed, I go into the bathroom, I drink some water, I vomit, then I—"

"Wait a minute," said the doctor. "You vomit? Every morning?"

"Why, yes," replied the boy. "Doesn't everyone?"

Those who have lived in fear think it natural. They are even more afraid of the unknown—security and peace.

Fear exists because love did not. The troubled person, as a child, felt unloved and unwanted. He believed his parents did not love him because there was something wrong with him. At times when he desperately needed them, he felt psychologically abandoned by his parents. And as an adult, he has never been able to overcome the feeling he is unlovable and a failure. He secretly holds little esteem for himself no matter how widely or wildly the world acclaims him or how many dollars he is able to collect.

The degree to which a man feels troubled is the degree to which he was deprived of love as a child.

"To a child, having no love is death," says Dr. John C. Thurrott, psychoanalyst.

He goes on to say, "Children should automatically receive love; ordinarily adults must merit it."

If children do not automatically receive love, they are troubled as children and troubled as adults. The love a child needs is a reassuring love born of happiness. It is not a demanding, possessive love created out of hunger. It is not the passionate love that flashes across movie screens. Nor is it the love that leads a parent to say or feel, "Be a good child or we won't love you."

Instead, it is a love that trusts, and in the trust there is tolerance and wisdom. It is deep, consistent. Parents who give this kind of love allow children to grow naturally and comfortably. They spin a cocoon of kindness in which the child may flourish and gain the strength that eventually leads to self-dependence.

Parents who cannot give love, through no fault of their own but because they received no love from their parents and so do not know what love is, push children in many directions, upsetting their natural growth. The children then carry through life a belligerent spirit that protests this tampering. They anticipate trouble when it does not exist.

A baby comes into the world helpless. He feels as though lost in the wildest jungle. He can do nothing except cry and suck. When his mother stands by, giving him love and attending to his needs, he feels secure and happy. He does not reason it out, but he knows, "I am loved. I am wanted. Someone is taking care of me."

But if his mother resents or neglects him, he is keenly aware of this disinterest or withdrawal. He feels, "I am not loved. No one cares about me. I may die." Unconsciously, those who are unloved feel their parents wish to murder them. If a baby is not loved, he may not be fed, and without food he will die. To survive, he may be forced into desperate devices which he feels will net him the love which means life. But in later years these devices bring only unhappiness, for they are built on fear, not love.

The wave on which troubles ride in adult life, even though we may not be aware of it, is this early fear of being left alone to die. To cope with this child-fear, a troubled person may go through torture after torture, to him preferable to what he feels meant death as a child.

The troubled live in ghost-fear from the unremembered but never-forgotten past. They are terrorized not alone by specific fears—fear of silence, fear of heights, fear of meeting people—but by an all-pervading fear which distorts and dramatizes the details of living. Everything becomes a matter of life and death.

Fearful, they turn to the world faces pockmarked with anger, which is their only hope for survival. Their lives could be described as "anger at work."

Unfortunately, anger is a boomerang. Anger makes the troubled feel guilty and then they become still angrier at feeling guilty, turning this desperate weapon constantly on themselves.

The anger also makes them feel ashamed and even more unworthy of love. They will not let anyone get close to them lest they reveal what they believe is a hideous self. They live tormented by fear.

CHAPTER 4

The Doors of Desperation Open

B u⊤ although the troubled try to hide from themselves and others what they feel is the hated self, part of them never lets them forget the fear or the anger. This is the "unconscious."

The unconscious, where much of the instinctual driving force of our life exists, is the storehouse of our memories of past events. We may compare the mind to an ocean. The surface is our conscious, the depths, our unconscious. Certain memories lie on the surface or near the surface while others are buried. If something comes along to stir up the deeper thoughts, like the wind on the ocean, our unconscious may become conscious.

Time causes us to forget some things. But others are forgotten because we cannot bear to remember them. It is normal to hide a certain amount in our unconscious. But the unconscious of the troubled person carries far more than an average load. This overburdening creates the inner suffering that may either sweep him like a fever or paralyze him like an icy chill.

The unconscious and conscious work in harmony in the untroubled. They work against each other in the troubled.

"I lie awake all night because I'm afraid my heart will stop beating," admitted one troubled man. His unconscious self was not trusting his unconscious to keep him alive because of his fear.

How do we know what lies in our unconscious?

A doctor named Sigmund Freud discovered how man could reach his unconscious so he might know against what he really struggled.

Freud fired the gun heard 'round the conscious world when he learned that men repress into their unconscious the knowledge of feelings and thoughts that cause pain.

He found out that the reasons we give for saying, thinking, feeling or doing certain things may not always be the real reasons. We fight knowing the real reasons because they too often touch on taboos we believe shameful—hatred, envy, incest, homosexuality.

[38]

Some critics charge that Freud did not discover any truth unknown to the Greek poets or Shakespeare. If he did not, he put that intuitive truth to use to help ease the pain of living. No one else, before or since, has explored man's inner suffering so deeply. This should rank Freud among the greatest of discoverers if we believe the poles of the self are as important as the North and South Poles.

Freud's life was dedicated to the troubled. He told a young writer, Bruno Goetz:

"My purpose is to help as well as I can the many people who today live internally in hell. Not in some hereafter but here on earth most people live in a hell. . . . My scientific findings, my theories and methods, aim at making them conscious of this hell so that they will be able to free themselves from it."

"The strongest character I ever met," was the description given Freud by the late Dr. Paul Federn during the dedication of Freud's statue at the New York Psychoanalytic Institute in 1947.

"One must think of Galileo, Cromwell, Zola, Jefferson, Lincoln, to find his equal," Dr. Federn said. "He was convinced that any knowledge of the truth enables us to fulfill better any task of civilization—be it medical, psychiatric, educational, individual or sociological. However painful it is first to accept the truth, illusions and rationalizations must be recognized and given up. Then only can we become able to use the truth and to cope with realities."

Today, civilization, perhaps in order to survive, is using

more of the "truth," realizing that troubled feelings may lead to the destruction of the world.

A bewildered observer at the 1952 national political conventions might have believed he had mistakenly wandered into a psychiatric conference. "Schizophrenic," "temperamentally unfit," "immature"—these words were spoken not by psychiatrists, but by candidates for the presidency of the United States.

Governor Adlai Stevenson, in his welcoming address to the Democrats, might have been talking to the troubled when he said to the nation:

"Self criticism is the secret weapon of democracy, and candor and confession are good for the political soul."

And again when he quoted St. Francis: "Where there is patience and humility, there is neither anger nor worry."

President Dwight D. Eisenhower, in his inaugural address, described what might well underlie the happiness of an individual as well as a nation:

". . . For this truth must be clear before us: whatever America hopes to bring to pass in the world must first come to pass in the heart of America.

"The peace we seek, then, is nothing less than the practice and fulfillment of our whole faith among ourselves and in our dealings with others. . . . More than escape from death, it is a way of life. More than a haven for the weary, it is a hope for the brave."

On sea as well as on land appears deeper understanding that there is part of man beyond his control that may drive him to fantastic deeds. Why did the minesweeper Hobson suddenly swerve left instead of right, as prearranged, and crash into the aircraft carrier Wasp?

"A trick of the subconscious mind" of the skipper might have been to blame, suggested Captain Burnham C. Mc-Caffree of the Wasp, at the Navy inquiry.

Lieutenant Commander William J. Tierney and 175 of his men went down with the Hobson in April, 1952, so there was no way of finding out what lay buried in the lost skipper's unconscious. But it was significant that Captain Mc-Caffree mentioned the subconscious as a possible cause of one of the fleet's most tragic peacetime accidents.

What has the unconscious to do with troubled feelings? The degree to which it rules us is the degree to which we are troubled. The heart of trouble is the carefully balanced seesaw between conscious and unconscious. If it tips too far, we are apt to suffer.

Behavior determined predominantly by conscious forces is "free," in the words of Dr. Lawrence Kubie, psychoanalyst. This kind of behavior is "flexible and realistic." It can be influenced by appeals to reason and feeling, by argument and exhortation, by success and failure, by rewards and punishments. It is "free to learn and to grow in wisdom and understanding," says Dr. Kubie.

But behavior determined predominantly by unconscious forces, whether or not it is conscious or unconscious behavior, such as the compulsive washing of hands (a conscious act), is "rigid and inflexible." It never learns from experience. It cannot be altered by argument or reason, persuasion

[41]

or exhortation, rewards or punishments, and not even by its own successes and failures.

Sometimes we are misled by what seems free behavior. We can understand, for instance, how a man who commits murder or suddenly appears to go mad is driven by his unconscious. He knows better, but something beyond his control "possesses" him.

It is not so easy to understand, however, that some who are successful according to society's standards, such as the business man who earns a million dollars, may be driven by their unconscious, although in another direction. They may also be deeply troubled.

For it is not alone what we do but how we do it that tells whether we are troubled. If we act out of desperation rather than choice, we are apt to be unhappy.

A man may paint magnificent pictures that the world admires, not because he enjoys painting but from inner frenzy. The life of Vincent Van Gogh and other troubled men who had to destroy themselves leads one to wonder if art is worth the price some artists pay for it.

Athletes who play the game not for the fun of it but because they *must* win, the movie stars who *must* achieve fame, the scholars who *must* excel intellectually, are unhappy. The *must* in a life shows its drivenness.

Those controlled by the unconscious make desperate decisions of which they are never sure. Afterwards they are tortured by the thought they should have done something else. It is an illusion that unhappy people choose for themselves. Their past chooses for them.

When the unconscious over-possesses someone, it signs a slow death warrant to his spirit. Powerful punishment is required to kill our will to live, for it is strong. It will undergo an intense psychic beating before it falls, defeated.

In most of us, the search to gain or regain the spirit goes on all our lives. Even though it may lie crumpled and dashed on the rocks of fear, enough of the spirit often survives to comfort and sustain if given love.

The spirit will revive as one comes to know and accept the inner self, or unconscious. As one becomes aware of what causes troubled feelings, one also finds out that the troubled feelings are unwarranted. They may once have been needed; now they are but the albatross.

A woman judge from Paris visited the Diagnostic Center at Menlo Park, New Jersey, a state institution for the study and treatment of some of the troubled. Here the drug, Sodium Pentothal, is sometimes used to help people recall events they have forgotten. She demanded of Dr. Ralph Brancale, the director, that she be given the drug, and, while under its influence, be allowed to talk freely.

"And I want a record made of *everything* I say," she ordered.

"You must have a clear conscience," Dr. Brancale remarked in wonder, for few voluntarily ask for the truth serum.

"Not at all," she replied. "It's only that I'm 3,000 miles from home. I want to hear the record. Then I want to smash it."

But we cannot smash our past, as revealed by our unconscious. Our aim should be not to destroy the past, but to know it as it really was and accept it. Then we will be less afraid, less troubled. This is the start of happiness.

The feel of trouble is not new. Trouble has tortured man since Adam and Eve. The causes of torment stand the same, no matter what culture or century. But today holds one great advantage over all eras. Those who lived before us were doomed to despair. They had no way of understanding their unhappiness.

Freud opened the doors that led to the secrets of desperation. He found a way to expose these secrets to the light of reason and thus give man the chance to live with himself, instead of trying to escape from himself.

Freud gave to everyman the right to become aware of inner agony. No longer were Hamlet and Orestes alone entitled to rave onstage, torn apart by pangs of anger and guilt. Each man stood privileged and even encouraged to look into his suffering if it meant stopping the war within and the war waged against the world.

No longer does man have to run away from what he feels is the sordid island of self.

No longer need he find it easier to communicate around the world than with his inner self.

No longer must he accept trouble as his cross to bear.

He can be helped to turn his eyes from the world outside to the world within. Thus he may gain a measure of vision and start to direct his destiny. He need no longer perish.

CHAPTER 5

This Thing Called Help

Some can face life without feeling overwhelmed. Others get along with advice from friends or relatives, ministers or doctors. But still others find no one who can help them to overcome despair.

The cause of their unhappiness is deeply hidden and they cannot reach it alone. For them, the journey into self—the most exciting, challenging voyage one can take—may require a guide.

Yet there is something about asking for professional help that terrifies many a man.

"I would rather die than ask someone to solve my problems," vehemently announced a lawyer who suffered acute heart trouble. He probably could have added years to his life if he sought help. But he was afraid.

The unhappy willingly gulp down the most dreadful concoction a doctor can dream up, or face without complaint the most serious assault on their body in the form of surgery, but one word about help for troubled feelings and they fly into panic.

Some who muster enough bravery to ask for help become terror-stricken when the hour arrives for them to start.

"The first time I visited a psychiatrist I had to walk around the block twice before I got up enough courage to ring the bell," confessed one man. "My heart pounded violently and I was in a cold sweat. When I finally got inside I coughed away the whole hour."

What is there about asking for help that creates such terror?

Men are afraid of what others will think if they confess they are troubled. Society scoffs at troubled feelings as a sign of weakness. When someone succumbs to the measles or the mumps, we do not blame him for his spots or his bumps. But somehow we hold men accountable for their failure to meet inner fear, as if they should know better.

They are afraid that because they ask for help others will think them queer, *à la* Sam Goldwyn, the movie producer, who is alleged to have remarked, "Anyone who goes to a psychiatrist ought to have his head examined."

A woman living in a midwestern city said wistfully, "I have never met anyone who accepts and understands why I am getting help. My friends think I'm crazy to want to be any different from the way I am."

It is ironic that society should call "crazy" those who seek help. And it is no wonder that some would rather be considered hardened criminals, drug addicts, sexually maladjusted, alcoholics or remain hopelessly crippled by physical illness than admit they are troubled.

The one who seeks help not only fears the censure of society but the censure of the one to whom he turns. It is as though he confesses, "My very being here is an admission I am helpless."

He fears confessing helplessness. No one likes to admit he does not understand himself or that he has failed to solve his own problems.

He has another overriding fear. He feels like the criminal who is warned: "Everything you say will be held against you." Unaware of what his crime is, he is afraid everything he says will be a revelation of guilt about this unknown but deeply felt crime.

He finds it difficult to tell someone else what he dares not tell himself. It is because feelings and thoughts proved so painful in the first place that he is troubled.

Many a man has sat for an hour saying little or nothing to the one giving help, even though he knows he pays a high price for silence. He cannot talk. He is afraid to talk because he may reveal too much about himself and run the risk of the other person's dislike.

He fears further hurt and rejection. He is afraid that the one who gives help will sit in judgment on him as his parents once did. He does not want to be criticized, judged or thought "bad." He wants to be cherished and accepted as he is.

Then, he fears the unknown and the intangible. An operation, a pill, an injection, an electric shock, even though painful, may be preferable to the risk of revealing thoughts and feelings in a way strange to him. The troubled fear to seek psychological help because they do not know what it is.

"What will he do to me?" one woman asked fearfully about a psychiatrist.

What is done *to* people? Nothing is done to them, but with them. They are given a sense of comfort and love so they may take heart and face themselves.

The one who gives help puts out a reassuring hand to the one who seeks help. The strength of this clasp enables the troubled to rise to their feet and stand alone.

The clasp holds the warmth of love. It says, "I believe in you. I have faith in you. I accept you as you are." It tells the troubled, "I know you have done what you have done in order to keep alive. I don't blame you for wanting to live. I want to help you live more easily."

This is help—not alone the exchange of spoken words but, more important, the exchange of unspoken words.

The intangible feelings that flow between the one who seeks help and the one who gives it are the stuff by which help succeeds or fails. These feelings add up to trust. It is through this trust that the troubled gain confidence. Because someone else believes in him, the troubled person starts to believe in himself.

When he comes for help, it is as though he pleads, "Please believe in me—no one ever has. Please trust me—no one ever has. Please love me—no one ever has." He seeks a love that will forgive him his anger and hate, recognizing it as the only way he knew to fight his fear. He seeks a love that will allow him to lose his loneliness. He searches for someone who will care enough about him so he may care for and trust himself.

But while he seeks love, at the same time he has difficulty accepting it. As he asks, "Please love me," he withdraws in self-hatred, thinking, "How could anyone love me?"

When the word "love" is used in giving help, it does not mean "love" in the man-woman sense. Rather, it is similar to the love of an understanding parent for a child. It is a guiding, ennobling love that asks nothing in return. It is a love without fear. It is a love that understands the sorrow that may be contained in a troubled life; a love content to wait for change, knowing the healing power of time if direction is true. It is the love that Virgil meant when he said, "Love conquers all," for it conquers even fear. It is a love that is "in itself both dynamic and therapeutic," as Dr. Douglas Darling, psychiatrist, puts it. Out of this love comes a second chance for the troubled.

The troubled need time to believe someone can love and accept them in this way. "If I couldn't trust my parents, who

[49]

were supposed to love me more than anyone else, how can I trust a perfect stranger?" they feel.

Sometimes only a stranger can supply the missing love. Sometimes it takes a stranger to be able to stand aside, observe, and know what a life needs to bring it fulfillment.

But this stranger must possess some important qualities if he is to help the troubled. It cannot be *any* stranger. It must be one who knows the essence of fear and how to displace it with safety. It must be a man able to give the one who seeks help a feeling of being respected, a feeling that there is dignity even in trouble.

It must be a man who loves himself. If a troubled person must gain love of self, then for him to acquire the feeling of love from someone else means that the one who gives help must have love of self. If he does not, he cannot bestow on anyone else a sense of being loved.

The feeling of love stems not so much from the words as the way they are spoken. The voice of the one who helps "is most effective when it is low and intimate, when his words allay the torture of conflict and the misery of insecurity," says Dr. Clarence Oberndorf, psychoanalyst.

In order for his words to accomplish this, he must be a man who has, in one way or another, faced his own inner self. He has no need to use those who seek help to ease his fear. He is able to put the troubled first. His life, in a sense, is dedicated to helping them.

This is not to say he cannot have a life of his own, but it is only when the needs of the troubled come before his own during working hours that he will be giving the best in him.

Some who work with the troubled are so dedicated they will spend many hours a day with one man if they feel he needs them.

Dr. Frieda Fromm-Reichmann, psychoanalyst, asked a woman who had been talking about the man who was helping her, "What is his name?"

The woman told her.

"I haven't heard of him," said Dr. Fromm-Reichmann thoughtfully.

"You probably haven't," said the woman. "He doesn't write learned papers or go to many meetings. He believes his job is to help people."

"God bless him!" said Dr. Fromm-Reichmann.

There are men and women throughout America who have faced themselves and come up with a fair share of inner peace. They are achieving remarkable results in their quiet, day-by-day work with the troubled.

They know the words and the music of help. They know the words so well they do not need such jargon as: "She is an orally regressed neurotic, masochistically attached to the image of her pre-oedipal mother."

They know this really means: "She is an unhappy person still searching for a good mother because she has never felt loved."

They do not confuse themselves or the troubled with esoteric language. They use the simple words: love, fear, hate, envy, rage.

"All the important words are four-letter words," remarked one psychiatrist.

An editorial in the Bulletin of the Menninger Foundation comments on the training of psychiatrists:

"It has been our experience that many residents in the early days of their training need to be directed first to a better acquaintance with such sources as the Bible, Aesop's Fables, Grimm's Fairy Tales and Dostoievski's novels rather than to technical treatises on Gestalt psychology and psychoanalysis."

Freud gave us an example of some of the important qualities needed by those who give help. An interesting story, up to now unpublished in this country, offers a new picture of Freud. It is told by Mr. Goetz, the young writer who sought Freud's assistance because he was suffering from facial neuralgia so severe he was forced to stay in a darkened room sometimes for weeks, as light caused such pain.

In his own words:

Freud approached me, shook hands with me, asked me to take a seat, and looked at me attentively. I looked into his wonderfully kind, warm, melancholy-knowing eyes. At the same time I had the feeling as if a hand had stroked fleetingly across my forehead—and the pains seemed wiped away.

"Oh," it went through my mind, "this is a sort of Indian medicine man. He doesn't need all his methods. He could as well say 'Abracadabra' and immediately one's heart would feel freer and one would feel better. This is the way a physician should be!" I had never before seen such a man. In the same moment I gained unconditional confidence in him. He sat silently for a few seconds smiling to himself. Then he said kindly:

"Let me get to know you a little. I have here a few of

your poems. Very nice—but incapsulated. You are hiding yourself behind your words instead of letting yourself be carried by them. Head up! You do not need to be afraid of yourself! . . . And now tell me something of yourself. In your verses, over and over the sea appears. Do you want to refer to anything symbolically? Or did you have anything to do with the sea in reality? From where, actually, do you come?"

I felt as if a dam had been broken. And before I knew how, I had told him the history of my whole life, had told him without restraint things about which I had not told anyone else. What sense would it have made to hide anything from him? Everything was known to him beforehand anyway.

For nearly a whole hour he listened without interrupting me and without looking at me. Sometimes he chuckled. At last he said:

"Now, my dear studious Goetz, I will not analyze you. Be blessed with your complexes. But for your neuralgia I will give you a *real* prescription."

He sat down at his desk. As he wrote, he remarked casually, "I have been told you have scarcely any money and are living skimpily. Is that true?"

I told him that my father could not pay for my education with his small salary as a teacher because there were still four younger children; thus I had decided to stand on my feet and was living from tutoring and occasional free-lancing for newspapers.

"Yes," he said, "strictness toward oneself has also its good sides. Yet one should not exaggerate it. When did you eat your last beefsteak?"

"I think four weeks ago."

"I thought this likely," he said and rose from the desk. "Here you have your prescription." He added some more dietetic suggestions and then became almost embarrassed. "You must not resent this, but I am a full-grown doctor and you are still a young student. Accept this envelope from me and permit me today to play the role of your father for a change. A small fee for the pleasure which you have given me with your verses and the story of your youth. Goodbye, and call me sometime again. My time is very much occupied but half an hour or even an hour can always be found for you. *Auf Wiedersehen!*"

And so he said goodbye to me. And imagine—when I opened the envelope at home I found 200 Kronen in it. I was in such an uproar—I had to weep.

Mr. Goetz reported that "the medicine which Freud prescribed" had such a good effect that his neuralgia disappeared within two weeks. One suspects the tears he shed because of Freud's kindness helped ease the pain.

The one who helps must have the skill of the artist and the knowledge of the scientist. One without the other does not work. He might have all the knowledge in the world but be missing understanding and compassion. Or he might be a warm, sympathetic person, yet not know how to help.

Essentially, those who give help must possess the quality of a healer. They have to bind the wounds of the psyche, soothe the jagged edges as they gently squeeze out the infection.

It is not easy to give the kind of love needed to help the troubled. It requires of a man the ability to give love even though he receives hatred in return. He is able to do this because he knows the hatred arises from fear. It also requires he be able to accept from others constant reminders of what may have been the pain in his own life.

Perhaps we may ask of each one who helps the troubled, in Shakespeare's words:

> Canst thou not minister to a mind diseas'd,
> Pluck from the memory a rooted sorrow,
> Raze out the written troubles of the brain,
> And with some sweet oblivious antidote
> Cleanse the stuff'd bosom of that perilous stuff
> Which weighs upon the heart?

The "sweet oblivious antidote" is, of course, love.

CHAPTER 6

Among Those Who Hold Out Hope

ONE woman will never forget a night not so long ago. All through it, she walked the floor, forcing back tears. She kept asking herself, "Where have I failed?"

That afternoon the school superintendent telephoned to inform her that her eight-year-old daughter, Mary, was a "problem." She could not get along with the other children. She had slapped one little girl several times and the girl's mother had called the school, demanding Mary be expelled.

"What shall I do?" asked Mary's mother, trembling.

"We suggest you get in touch with a family agency and see a social worker," said the superintendent.

"Could you give me the name of one?" asked the mother, also wanting to ask what a social worker was, but not daring.

The superintendent named an agency, saying, "Their social workers have helped a number of our children."

"I don't have much money," said the mother, thinking of the $80 a week her husband earned on which she fed and clothed her family of six.

"They will charge little or nothing," said the superintendent.

After her sleepless night, the mother called the agency. She explained what had happened. That day a young woman came to visit her, started her talking about Mary and other members of the family.

Once a week for six months, the young social worker came to call. At the end of this time the mother was amazed at how differently she felt about herself and her daughter.

"It's hard to put it into words," she said. "Six months ago I felt low. I felt I was to blame for Mary's failure. Now I know it wasn't entirely my fault. I also see where I can help Mary."

She went on, "It's difficult when you have four children to know what to do sometimes. I never knew each one of my children was so different. I always thought of Mary as being the strong child in the family. She was the one who never got sick. She's skinny but strong. I'm always having to take care of the others."

She added softly, "But now I see Mary needs attention

in another way. I left her alone too much. She was feeling out of the family."

The door opened and Mary, an attractive, energetic little girl, raced in. "I need a penny, Ma," she said. Then she asked in that studied careless tone which masks seriousness, "Are you going to help me with my homework tonight?"

"Sure, sure," said her mother. When Mary left the room, clutching the penny, the mother said in quiet excitement, "Did you hear that? She would never let me touch her homework before. And it's all because that nice young woman, that social worker, has helped me to know what was wrong."

Social workers are among those helping the troubled. We have five groups in this country who give professional help—social workers, psychologists, psychiatrists, psychoanalysts and lay analysts. Psychoanalysts and psychiatrists possess medical degrees, the others do not.

Just as there are different depths to trouble, so there are different depths to help. Help may be divided into two main categories—supportive or mildly corrective, and deep. Sometimes these overlap; there are also many degrees between the two extremes.

In mildly corrective or supportive help, the troubled discuss current problems, let the past lie, and do not probe into the unconscious. They do not want or need to stir up the deeper currents. In deep therapy, called psychoanalysis, they explore the unconscious.

There are 75,000 social workers in the nation. They give supportive help, ranging from getting money for those in economic distress or finding summer camps for children, to aiding people with the various problems of living. Of these social workers, 4,500 have had training in psychiatric social work and are qualified to work with a psychiatrist in the treatment of a troubled person.

Social workers are found, among other places, in family agencies, mental hospitals, general hospitals, courts, clinics and prisons. The agencies in which they work charge slight fees or no fees.

At family agencies they see the troubled first, asking questions to find out how serious their problems may be.

"What seems to be the matter?" a social worker asked a mother who came with her ten-year-old daughter to the New York Catholic Charities.

"Our doctor told me to bring Jane because she stutters so in class, and he can't find anything physically wrong with her," said the mother, sitting tensely in the chair.

"Does she stutter badly?" asked the social worker, looking at Jane, who was tall for her age and tried to hide her height by hunching her shoulders.

"She gets all red and sometimes no sound at all comes when she tries to speak," said the mother. "The school said, though, that she is polite and obedient and never disobeys the teacher."

The social worker, after questioning the mother further, gave her report to the agency's psychiatrist. He studied it and concluded that Jane's stuttering might be psychosomatic (bodily illness with an emotional cause). He noted that the stuttering first appeared when Jane's younger sister was born.

He recommended that both Jane and her mother visit the social worker regularly and talk over their troubles.

After eight months of help, Jane and her mother seemed more at ease with each other. Jane was also standing up straighter.

"Jane stutters much less," the social worker reported. "She holds her own now with her younger sister of whom she was always afraid. She is able to express more of her feelings." She added with a laugh, "When she tells off her sister, she doesn't stutter a bit."

In talking about how she felt, the mother commented, "For the first time in my life, I have been able to think out loud with someone else. No one ever listened to me before. I realize how I had been favoring the little one over Jane. Now Jane seems more demonstrative—she's part of this world."

A young man heard that Roosevelt Hospital in New York had opened a clinic where the troubled might be helped. He went to the hospital, was interviewed by a social worker.

He explained, "I have a cough and I can't sleep nights. When I walk down the street I feel as though the buildings of the city were about to fall on me."

"Were you born here?" asked the social worker.

"No—I grew up in a mining town near Pittsburgh," he said. "My parents didn't seem to care what I did, so when I was sixteen I headed for New York. Now I'm twenty-six and don't seem to be getting anywhere in life."

"What do you do for a living?" asked the social worker.

"I play in a small band occasionally, work days slinging

hash in a restaurant," he said. "It's tough going when you can't sleep."

"Would you like to see our psychiatrist?" asked the social worker. "He might be able to help you feel better."

He looked alarmed. "I've never been near a psychiatrist. They're for queer people, aren't they?"

She smiled. "They're to help people with little difficulties, too."

"I don't think I want to see him—unless I have to," he said.

"You don't *have* to do anything," she said. "But would you like to take a few tests from our psychologist to find out if you have some hidden abilities?"

He agreed. The psychologist gave him several aptitude tests. They showed he had artistic talent.

"I always liked to draw," the young man said excitedly, when he learned this.

"You might be able to use your skill to greater advantage if you talked to the psychiatrist," suggested the social worker. "He's really a wonderful person. You ought to be glad to have the chance to get his help."

"All right," the young man said. "My cough doesn't seem to be getting any better. Maybe he can tell me what to do."

His first visit with the psychiatrist led to a second and a third. He kept coming back once a week for a year, during which time he talked about his unhappy childhood and his feelings about his parents. At the end of that time, his cough had disappeared, he could sleep at night, and he was well on his way to a career in commercial art. The clinic team—

social worker, psychologist and psychiatrist—had helped him get on his feet, emotionally speaking.

Social workers also help overcome fear of illness and operations. A nine-year-old girl returned to Roosevelt Hospital for a check-up after her appendix was taken out. As she walked down the corridor, she recognized the social worker on the hospital's social service staff who had talked to her during her stay at the hospital, helping to lessen the terror of the operation.

"Hello," called out the child eagerly. "Is today visiting day at the hospital?"

"Yes, dear," replied the social worker.

"Well, can I come and visit with you even if I'm not sick any longer?" she asked wistfully.

Roosevelt Hospital is one of two in New York State that are part of a new experiment in emotional health. The State Department of Mental Hygiene is giving funds to provide psychological help for the troubled, both those confined in the hospital and those who come to the hospital for a few hours a day, in order to prevent more serious emotional disturbances later on.

Some children have been brought in complaining of stomach or head hurts, yet nothing organically wrong can be found. One child suffered vomiting spells without any apparent physical cause. In talking to her, the social worker found out she was so frightened of her mother and older brother that she did not want to go home after school. The vomiting would start after she reached home.

Social workers play an important part in the institutions

that take care of our emotionally disturbed children who get in trouble with the law. They help "the quiet ones," as well as those not so "quiet," who, unable to hold in their fury at a world they never made, explode in wrath.

Ten-year-old John Jones was sent to Wiltwyck, a private institution for delinquent boys in the wooded foothills of the Catskills, across the Hudson River from Hyde Park, New York. He was committed there by the Children's Court of New York City for truancy, stealing and refusing to obey his parents.

A few days after he arrived, he stole three knives in twenty-four hours, threatening to kill his teacher and a classmate. Each time one knife was taken away from him, he stole another.

"I'll keep on getting them, too," he boasted. "I have to kill someone."

The social work staff, led by Ernst Papenek, the director of the school, held a conference to discuss if it was safe to keep the boy. They knew if he attacked anyone, the court would send him to a mental hospital or an institution where he would be less likely to get help.

They realized the boy had reason for anger. His father had always punished him severely for disobeying (John had said angrily, "I hate all men!"). They knew the classmate he threatened to kill was the one who told the school authorities he had stolen the knives, and that the teacher he threatened had tried to discipline him after he stole a roll of cellophane tape. They decided to gamble that he could be helped by kindness.

Mr. Papenek took the boy into his office, said, "Look, John, we know you feel angry. We still love you. We want you here. But you must help us, too. You can't go around threatening to kill people. What if we all did that?"

The boy said nothing. Mr. Papenek held out a piece of candy. The boy seemed undecided whether to accept it, then quickly snatched it.

In the next few weeks the staff's courageous decision paid off. The teacher whom John had threatened to kill asked him to help stack books on the classroom shelves. John did this willingly, then wanted to know what more he could do. He forgot about stealing knives. No longer did the staff have to watch him night and day to protect the other boys.

One social worker got John interested in boxing (giving him a chance to express constructively some of his anger) and dancing. He became comfortable enough with the other boys to take part in an impromptu show.

"He now wants to get attention—which is basically a need for love—by pleasing, instead of killing," Mr. Papenek said at a meeting where John's progress was discussed. "We've got him on the right track. But he needs direction, as well as attention. He cannot fight his way out alone. He does not know where to go."

He was helped to find out where to go during the next few months. He accepted the guidance of the social worker who showed him how to box. He became friends with the classmate he had once threatened to kill. The change in him was marked.

The blind may lead the blind successfully. At The Lighthouse of the New York Association for the Blind, blind social workers who are also teachers help other blind persons too troubled to leave their homes.

One of the social workers was telling another about the progress of a 45-year-old woman. Once she held an important community job. Following an operation, she became completely paralyzed on the right side, had difficulty speaking, and went blind.

"I've been teaching her how to make a leather belt," said the first social worker.

"With her left hand?" asked the second in surprise.

"Well, she uses her teeth a little to help out," said the first.

The second social worker described how he had gone into the home of a 22-year-old youth who could barely see and soon would be totally blind.

"He hasn't accepted his blindness yet," said the social worker. "He doesn't want to associate with blind people. He is withdrawn and suspicious of everyone. But I think, given time, we can help him."

Social work is the one institution that helps people use other institutions in our society, according to Helen Witmer, social work leader. It is the bridge whereby people can find their way to what they seek, be it a foster home, a baby to adopt, a summer camp, a way to earn money to get through college, a home for the aged, or psychiatry.

Social workers consider "the whole person," even though they may deal with only one part. For instance, a couple asked a private family agency to help them pay rent because they both were out of work.

"If we help you with your rent, what can you do to assure us that it will be different next month, that you will be able to pay yourselves?" asked the social worker.

"What do you mean?" asked the husband.

"Why have you both been out of jobs, what are you doing to get work? Have you come here, perhaps, because of other problems?" asked the social worker.

The couple started to think about these questions. They came back to visit the social worker once a week for three months to discuss troubles other than the rent. At the end of that time, both were working.

Social work aims at an immediate, practical end. The social worker is aware of deeper problems but focuses only on the immediate ones—easing the fear of a family upset by a death, aiding a handicapped person to start a new job—giving specific help.

Sometimes a social worker provides a prelude to psychiatry. He recognizes when a troubled person needs to face deeper fears and he may be able to make it easier for the troubled to accept psychiatry or psychoanalysis.

A new development is that of private practice for social workers who see the troubled in their offices, charging them fees. They work closely with psychiatrists or psychoanalysts in each instance. In an issue of the News-Letter put out by the American Association of Psychiatric Social Workers, Rowena Ryerson and Elizabeth Weller of New York describe a service in which they offer private help to the troubled. The extent and depth of the help depends on the nature of the problem, the person's condition and capacity to use help, and the realistic limits "set by ethical and professional considerations," they stated.

The psychological demands made on social workers today call for their understanding themselves so they can understand others, says Charlotte Towle, one of the leaders in social work education.

Several schools of social work place special emphasis on the student's fitness for the profession, including The New York School of Social Work and The School of Social Work at Adelphi College, Garden City, Long Island.

"We believe that one of the ways social work can be best advanced is to see that those who are to help others give this help with understanding and sympathy," explained Alexander Handel, dean of Adelphi School of Social Work.

Another group which gives supportive help are the psychologists. Because of the growing demand for help, the psychologists of the nation have, in a sense, come out of the laboratory to meet the people. While many still do research (the "pure" science, as distinguished from the "applied") or teach in colleges and universities, an increasing number are dealing with emotional problems.

Psychologists, who have a degree in psychology, help both in private practice and in such community facilities as clinics, hospitals and family agencies. There are 11,000 of them who belong to the American Psychological Association and an estimated 7,000 more, some of whom do not meet the association's standards. Of the 11,000 members of the association, about 40 per cent are "clinical psychologists" who, through tests and verbal help, give aid to the troubled. When seen in their offices, they charge an average of $10 a visit. They may be visited for one session or over a period of weeks or months, depending on the troubled person's need.

The "clinical psychologists," those who work most closely with the psychiatric profession, find out through tests how troubled people may be and the depth of help they need. The two main tests are the Rorschach and the Thematic Apperception Test, known as TAT.

The latter is designed to draw out what a troubled person may be thinking of consciously and unconsciously. He is shown a series of pictures and asked to relate a story about each one.

"Tell us a story based on this picture," one psychologist asked a woman, showing her a woman standing alone, holding her hand over her eyes.

"She is crying because her son has left her," said the woman. "She doesn't understand why he's gone but he has. They had a terrible fight in which he threatened to kill her." (Later it developed this had happened between her and her son a week before.)

The Rorschach or "ink blot" test, as it is popularly known, consists of ten separate ink blots. The troubled person is asked to describe what he sees in the blots or any part of them.

One eleven-year-old boy, tested by Dr. Molly Harrower, clinical psychologist, looked at the blots and said, "This is the picture of a boy who has just taken something that he wants away from another."

His twin brother, tested an hour later, remarked, looking at the same blot, "This is the picture of a boy who has just had his things taken away from him."

Each boy gave a clue to his psychological world. The aggressive twin habitually snatched toys from his brother.

Just as, from a small smear of blood comes an accurate blood count, so, from a small look into a person's reactions, may come an accurate appraisal of his emotional make-up, says Dr. Harrower. Each person as he looks at the blots constructs "part of a world along the lines on which he is wont to experience and organize things in his everyday life."

In a recent book, *Appraising Personality*, written in the form of dialogue between psychologist and physician, Dr. Harrower explains what a clinical psychologist does and presents case histories. For instance, the psychologist says:

"I spent the day testing a boy in his second year of medical school who had suddenly begun to do very badly in his studies."

Tests showed that the young student might have a brain tumor. An electroencephalogram confirmed the findings. The psychologist commented:

". . . This finding is perhaps one in a thousand cases. However, a psychologist working in a neurological ward comes across this type of psychological finding frequently. In the ordinary run-of-the-mill of general practice, this is naturally very unusual."

It might have been easy to have "overplayed" the idea that

some psychological disturbance was at the root of the boy's trouble, the psychologist said. He probably had emotional difficulties, "as who does not?"

"But I think the psychological tests may have saved considerable time since they highlighted so clearly that some organic condition was present."

An increasing number of psychologists are helping the troubled with marital, sex and other personal problems. Some give vocational and aptitude tests.

One man, dissatisfied with his job in an insurance company, went to a psychologist and, as a result of tests, found that the hours he puttered around with tools were not wasted. He showed a real skill in designing machinery. He got a job with an industrial concern and was responsible for several important inventions.

Psychologists are finding a niche in the industrial field. Dr. Edward M. Glaser, consulting psychologist to several large business firms, explains:

"There is need for the application of psychology to the normal human relations problem of people bouncing against each other in an organization. If the psychologist can help people further and faster to develop their best potential and can help blend good manpower into smoother teampower, then the organization should become more productive, more stable and more profitable."

This, in turn, is of triple benefit, he maintains—to the customers who pay lower prices; to the employees who receive higher earnings and find more congenial relationships in their work, and to the owners who derive greater profit from superior productivity.

But Dr. Glaser puts the happiness of the individual first. He believes productivity will take care of itself if the person feels happy. In his evaluation of a person, if there is need for deep therapy or further counseling, he will advise it.

Even the sports world is taking to psychology. Psyche triumphed over physique when the St. Louis Browns hired a psychologist to try to bring them out of their slump. Some sports writers hinted their doubt whether even a psychoanalysis for each player could help the Browns.

Sometimes in a broad sense, psychologists help men understand their fears. Michael B. Dunn, a clinical psychologist, received a telephone call from the parents of a boy whom he had once treated at a private school for emotionally disturbed children.

The boy, now a student at a western university, had entered a house to burglarize it. He wandered into a bedroom where two girls were sleeping. One of them awoke, saw him and screamed. He turned on her, beat her over the head with a pistol, seriously injuring her, and fled.

The police arrested him the following morning. He admitted, when confronted with evidence, that he had committed the crime, saying he could not explain why, and had no recollection of the act.

The frantic parents begged Dr. Dunn to come West and testify before the court in behalf of their boy.

"I went out expecting the worst," Dr. Dunn said. "The

community was highly aroused over the assault. The local and state newspapers had carried much sensational publicity."

When his time came to testify, Dr. Dunn took the stand. Quietly and with conviction, he described the boy's loneliness and rejection as a child, how he had never felt any sense of belonging to his family or himself. His parents put him in one private institution after another for twelve years of his life, although he could just as well have lived at home. His father, who held a nationally important job, could afford the expense of private institutions.

Dr. Dunn threw away the notes he had written on the train going West, and spoke from the emotion of the moment. He gave judge and jury a look into the soul of a tormented boy who had to resort to stealing and violence because he felt no one loved or wanted him.

When the trial ended, the jury, instead of committing the boy to a penal institution, decided he should receive further help with his emotional problems.

Dr. Dunn returned East but he did not leave the case behind. In the next few months, the judge and several members of the jury wrote him lengthy letters pouring forth some of their own emotional turmoil. The boy's plight and Dr. Dunn's interpretation of it had made them aware of some of their troubled feelings. They were less afraid to ask for help and understanding for themselves.

Dr. Dunn had helped this western town know some of the reasons why men commit crimes. Its reaction bore out what

Dr. Leonard Mayo, child welfare authority, said recently, that "man is showing more love for his fellow man."

Man is able to show love if he knows what creates hate. And social workers and psychologists are among those helping him to know.

CHAPTER 7

Psychiatry—Not the Couch, But the Chair

A WIFE was complaining to her husband over the supper table about the day's calamities.

"It isn't enough that my maid walks out without a second's notice, but Richard comes home from school with a report card full of D's, and Mother calls up and—"

Her husband looked at her, said wearily, "Tell it to a psychiatrist."

In a sense, this has become the twentieth-century substitute for "Tell it to the Marines!"

Just as the Marines are expected to wade in and conquer the enemy, so are psychiatrists expected to help conquer the enemy, unhappiness.

One psychiatrist described a day in his office. He said he thought it fairly typical.

His first patient was a woman whose husband had died a year previously. She explained she was worried about her seventeen-year-old son.

"He doesn't want to go out with his friends," she said. "He stays home and studies. It's all I can do to get him to go to school."

"Has he always been that way?" the psychiatrist asked.

"Much more so since his father died," the mother said.

The psychiatrist was silent. She went on, bitterly, "Since Joe died, my problems have increased. We have to live much more economically. I have to handle my son all by myself. It—" She bit her lips.

"It isn't easy," the psychiatrist said gently.

"I have so many feelings about Joe," she said. "Now that he's gone, I regret many things I didn't do for him—things I know would have made him happy. But it seemed I couldn't do them. He so often set out to antagonize me and I would freeze up."

She started talking about her husband, whom she had not loved. She confessed she felt guilty about his death.

"In a way, I feel responsible for his dying," she said in a whisper.

[76]

"You are not to blame," the psychiatrist told her. "No one person need feel responsible for another's death. That's taking too much upon the self."

They talked more about the son. The psychiatrist suggested she hold parties at the house for his friends, encourage him to go out with girls. She left, after making an appointment for the following week.

The second patient was a man the psychiatrist had been seeing once a week for four months. When he first came, he was a serious alcoholic. He was gradually giving up liquor; occasionally he would go on benders but not to the extent he did formerly.

"It's a funny thing, doc," he said to the psychiatrist. "My confidence that I can go without alcohol comes and goes in spurts. Sometimes I *know* I don't have to have the stuff, but then something happens and I find myself at a bar ordering a drink. I can't seem to control my desire."

"In time, perhaps, you will be able to," the psychiatrist said. "You're doing much better."

"I'd do a hell of a lot better if my wife didn't nag me," he said angrily. "She treats me like an imbecile. You'd think I didn't have a brain in my head."

"It's difficult for those who don't drink to understand those who drink too much," the psychiatrist said. "Have you tried to understand her point of view? She doesn't like to see you drunk, you know."

"I don't like the spectacle I make of myself when I'm drunk," he said sullenly.

"Then why do you drink so much?" the psychiatrist asked.

[77]

"I guess to forget certain things," he replied.

"What things?"

"A job I don't like, the feeling I've failed my wife and my mother and father, the fact that I'm not earning as much money as some of the guys I went to college with."

"Are those the important things in life?" the psychiatrist asked.

"I don't know *what's* important," he said.

"Let's find out what's important to you," said the psychiatrist. "When you were in school what did you want to be?"

The man began to reminisce how he once dreamed of writing. He recalled how excited he was when he was chosen editor of the college paper. But his father insisted he take over the family insurance business. He had worked in his father's office ever since college.

At the end of the hour he was in the middle of a tirade against parents who throttle their children's ambitions. As he rose from the chair, he half-smiled, said, "You know your business all right. I haven't ever talked about these feelings. But I guess I better haul 'em out and look at 'em since they appear to have been burning me up over the years. See you next week."

He was followed by a woman of twenty-eight who had trouble holding a job. She had worked in seven advertising agencies in a year. Each time she would get bored and leave. She had been coming to see the psychiatrist once a week for a month.

"I don't think you're doing me any good," she told him.

"But I might as well be here as roaming the streets looking for another job."

"Why don't you use to good advantage the time you spend here?" he suggested. "Let's not waste it. After all, you're paying money for help."

"I don't think you can help me," she said. "I'm here as a last resort. I must be able to hang on to a job. I can't depend on my parents to help me out financially all my life."

"Perhaps you really don't want to work," said the psychiatrist.

She looked at him in surprise. "I've always planned a career. I've always wanted to be independent."

"Independent of what?"

She did not reply. Then she burst out, "Do you think I *like* taking money from them?"

"Them?"

"My mother and father. They begrudge me every nickel they give me."

"Yet, paradoxically, you manage to keep enough out of work so you must take money from them in order to live," the psychiatrist said. "Why do you suppose you do that?"

The girl half-smiled. "I don't want to take anything from them and yet I want to take everything from them. Is that it?"

"Why don't you tell me how you really feel about them?"

"I wish I knew," the girl said. "I wish I knew."

"Let's try to find out," he said.

In the following half-hour the girl talked about her mother and father more frankly than she ever had before. When her time was up, she said, "Some of the pieces are starting to

come together. I still think you can't help me very much—
but let's give this a whirl and see where I come out."

The next patient was a woman complaining of severe
headaches. This was her first appointment. She spent twenty
minutes describing her visits to endless doctors, none of whom
had been able to cure her headaches.

"They started about half a year ago, right here," she said,
pressing the center of her forehead. "They pain me so I
can't do the housework. I can't sleep, I'm not hungry, I can
hardly see at times."

"They started about half a year ago?" the psychiatrist
asked.

"Yes," said the woman.

"Did you ever have them before?"

"Once, when I was in high school and failed a Latin examination. I got a dickens of a spanking from my father and
had the same kind of headache," she recalled.

"Do you have a feeling you're failing in anything now?"
he asked.

The woman's eyes filled with tears. She pulled a handker-
chief from her pocketbook and blew her nose. Then she said,
"You're very astute."

"What happened six months ago?" he asked.

"My husband came home and told me he was in love with
another woman," she said quietly. "And I don't know what
to do about it."

"Does he want a divorce?"

"He hasn't said so, which makes me think maybe we have

a chance of making the marriage work. I wish I knew where I failed."

The rest of the session was spent talking about her relationship with her husband, whom, she said, she had never understood and who had never understood her. As she left, she said, "I'd like to make a go of this marriage if I possibly can."

"If you want to, and will honestly face some things in it, you may make it work," the psychiatrist said.

After lunch he saw a twelve-year-old boy accompanied by his mother, a tight-lipped, reserved woman who explained, "Tom's flunking all his classes at school and the teacher says he needs a psychiatrist."

The psychiatrist asked her to leave the room while he talked to Tom. The boy sat across the desk from him.

"Don't you like school, Tom?" he asked.

"Yeah, it's all right," said the boy, his eyes nervously scanning the room.

"But you don't study for classes—how can you expect to get passing marks?"

"So I don't pass," he replied flippantly. "The worst she can do is not let me go to camp this summer. She's always whipping me with that."

Then he added, "And *he* will slap me some more. I can take that. It don't hurt too much." But muscles in his face jerked as though remembering familiar pain.

"Don't you want to get through school so you can go on to college and then get out into the world?" asked the psychiatrist.

The boy said nothing. His right hand went up to his face and patted it gently.

After a few more questions, the psychiatrist asked his nurse to show Tom some magazines and called in the mother.

"Your boy seems pretty troubled," he said. "Can you afford to send him to a psychoanalyst for more intensive help?"

"I don't know anything about psychoanalysts," she said, showing no more emotion than if he had told her to buy some aspirin.

"Tom needs to unburden himself of some deep feelings," he said. "I think it would reward you well in the long run if you would send him to Dr. Smith. If you agree, I could call him up and see if he has the time."

The mother's face was still expressionless. "If you say so," she said. "I came to you because you're the expert. We will do anything that will help Tom pass his examinations. His father insists his marks come before everything else."

"Perhaps that is one reason Tom is flunking," the psychiatrist said.

For the first time her eyes showed feeling. They softened. "I can understand that," she said slowly. "But I don't know how to help the boy."

"You helped by coming here," said the psychiatrist. "I'll call Dr. Smith and let you know if he's available. If he isn't, we'll get someone else."

"Thank you," said the mother, her face again expressionless as she walked out of the room.

Then a girl of twenty-five entered, an attractive, nervous

young woman. As she sat in the chair, she kept fussing with her pocketbook.

"I'm here because you helped my friend, Martha Jones," she said brusquely.

"Martha helped herself," the psychiatrist said. "I only encouraged her to do what she knew was right for her."

"I don't know what is right," she said, as though to herself.

She went on, "A good friend of mine has asked me to marry him and I'm not sure what to do about it. I'd like to get married but something seems missing between us. There's no umph. He's a wonderful guy, bright as they come. I'm very fond of him but he's not inspiring. He doesn't make my heart beat faster."

"Yet you like being with him?"

"Yes—but then I haven't had the chance to be with many men," she said. "I feel as if I want to explore further before settling down, yet I'm afraid I may not get another chance to marry if I don't accept Peter."

"You're young yet," the psychiatrist said. "Why do you feel in such a rush about getting married?"

"All my friends are married," she answered quickly. "I feel like the last spinster. It's humiliating to go to their homes and see all their children. I feel so jealous. Now here's a chance to have a home of my own and yet—" She sighed.

"You should marry a man because you love him, not for what he can give you that might change your life," the psychiatrist said. "If you marry him to solve problems that exist inside yourself, your marriage is apt to be unhappy."

[83]

"Like all the others I know," she said bitterly.

"Just because others are unhappy doesn't mean you have to be," he said.

"What will I do about Peter?" she wailed.

"What do you want to do?"

"If I knew, I wouldn't be here. I'm going crazy trying to decide."

Then she asked defiantly, "Do you think I'm crazy?"

"Why do you ask?" His tone was calm, sympathetic.

"Because all my life my mother has called me crazy. 'That crazy child of mine,' she says to company, even now." The girl's pocketbook fell to the floor. She did not notice it.

"I don't think you're crazy," said the psychiatrist. "I think you're caught in the conflict of what you feel you should do and what you feel you want to do, but that's not unusual in this society of ours."

"Why do you suppose she calls me crazy?" asked the girl.

"Parents sometimes don't think as clearly as they should," he said. "You mustn't take as gospel everything your mother says."

"I've never dared question her," the girl said, her eyes widening.

"How does she feel about Peter?" the psychiatrist asked.

"She likes him," the girl complained. "And perhaps that's one reason I've had so much trouble deciding about him. If she likes him, something must be wrong with him."

"Perhaps your mother isn't wrong about everything," the psychiatrist said.

"I still don't know what to do," the girl said, picking up her pocketbook.

"Why don't you come back next week and we'll talk some more?" he suggested.

"Martha came here for quite a while, didn't she? All right." She turned at the door and said abruptly, "Thank you."

She was followed by the final patient of the day, a middle-aged man who had been seeing the psychiatrist for six months. Married three times, when his third marriage appeared to be breaking up, he sought help.

His wife was also a patient of the psychiatrist's, visiting him another day in the week.

"We're getting along much better," said the man as he sat down. "We're not comparing notes any more on what takes place here. I think that's a good sign. We're starting to live with each other, not existing to torment each other."

The psychiatrist smiled. "I have a hunch any two people who are not too repulsive to each other can make a go of it, if they'll work hard enough at the marriage," he said.

"Who wants to work at marriage?" asked the man. "Shouldn't marriage be enjoyed?"

"Yes—but sometimes you don't get something for nothing," said the psychiatrist.

"What a price I'm paying!" sighed the man. "Alimony to wife numbers one and two. I can't afford to get divorced again."

"You won't solve anything by getting divorced again. And think how satisfied you'll feel if you make this one work."

[85]

"This week she really was nice to me," he said grudgingly. "She put herself out to get all the food I like and—say— what's happening to her? What are you doing to her?"

"I'm not doing anything *to* her," said the psychiatrist. "She's just feeling freer with you. And you with her. It takes two, you know, both to make a fight and to get along."

"She's changing, somehow," the husband said, almost admiringly. "She's like the old gal I married."

"You're changing, too," said the psychiatrist.

"Me?" He appeared surprised. Then he said, embarrassedly, "You know, I feel better after I come here and get things off my chest. I know half the time you don't listen—"

"But I do," said the psychiatrist. "Even to those things you don't want me to hear."

"Okay, then, you listen." He grinned. "It's such a relief to have someone to talk to about the damned fool things people do. Now today, at the office—"

He started describing some of the day's events that had made him nervous. He talked for the full hour. As he got up he said, "Darned if I'm going to let these things upset me so much. I should be man enough to take a little worry. See you next week for another East Lynne episode."

In the last fifteen years psychiatrists have moved from mental hospitals, in which most of them originally worked, out into the communities. About half the country's psychiatrists now help the less troubled.

You go to a psychiatrist, rather than a psychoanalyst, when you do not need, or do not want, to look deeply into the self. You go either to try to find the answer to a specific problem that bothers you, or because you feel tense, worried or insecure and do not know why.

Instead of lying on a couch, as with an analyst, you sit in a chair facing the psychiatrist. You talk about what disturbs you. The psychiatrist listens, helps you discover how you feel about your problems and what you want to do about them.

Although a psychiatrist usually does not help the troubled to explore the unconscious, he is aware of its force in a life. In guiding a man, he knows and respects hidden fears. He eases them by reassurance and kindliness. He may suggest changes that will make living more comfortable.

One young man told a psychiatrist that he did not know what was wrong with him but he found life intolerable. He described depressions which made it impossible for him to work.

"Are you married?" asked the psychiatrist.

"No. My father is dead and I live with my mother," said the young man.

He started talking about his mother in an adoring, worshipful way. He said, at one point, "She doesn't like my bringing girls to the house."

The psychiatrist asked the young man if he could afford to live by himself.

"I guess so," he replied. "But it would be hard on Mother. She's all alone."

"It will be harder for you if you continue living with her," said the psychiatrist. "You don't seem to have much of a life of your own.

At first the young man was upset at the suggestion he leave his mother. But after seeing the psychiatrist several times, he made up his mind to live alone.

The psychiatrist did not attempt to discuss the intense feelings the young man had about his mother. Instead, he suggested the young man move, believing he would feel less depressed if he were not constantly around his mother.

It is vital for the troubled not to face feelings that frighten them until they feel comfortable enough to handle them. There are some who can take only superficial help at first. Others can never accept more than superficial help because the pain of the psychic probing is too great.

Some may tell a psychiatrist they want relief from the pain of the moment—inability to sleep, a stomach ache, the death of a parent—when they really want or need help with the whole of living. The psychiatrist knows when someone can take more intensive help.

Sometimes he is able to lay the groundwork for its acceptance, helping the troubled lose fear of the search into self. He may refer them to an analyst when he thinks they are ready.

Or, if he feels someone is too frightened even for superficial help, he may resort to pills. One reputable psychiatrist told of a man who walked into his office deeply depressed.

"Last time I had this depression, ten years ago, the psychiatrist gave me a pill and I got well and never had another until just now," said the man.

So the psychiatrist gave him a pill. "This man was telling me what he came expecting and I knew he couldn't take anything more," he said. "He called a week later and told me he was completely out of the depression."

Some of the troubled ask only that physical symptoms disappear. Three or four sessions may be all they need. One woman who had a constant headache talked to the psychiatrist once a week for four weeks solely about how much she hated her mother-in-law. Then she called up to say, "I don't have to see you any more. My headache is gone."

The psychiatrist aims primarily to relieve current distress. He may do this by suggesting a change of environment, as did the psychiatrist who advised the young man to move away from his mother.

After several visits with a man they feel is wise and compassionate, some gain enough faith in themselves to reach decisions about problems that have troubled them. Some want only confirmation they are doing the right thing.

Asked why people go to psychiatrists, one psychiatrist replied, "Some want to be told they are not going crazy—and who better than a psychiatrist can tell them that? When they get the reassurance, they feel better."

Just talking things over with someone trustworthy may help the troubled feel better. The knowledge, too, that there is a kindly person from whom they may seek help if life becomes too full of dread, is in itself reassuring.

Psychiatrists have a medical degree, and special and extensive training in emotional problems. They may be seen in private offices where they charge from $10 to $25 a visit (the average is $15) and they also work in mental hospitals, family agencies, general hospitals, clinics, courts, prisons—wherever there are troubled persons.

We had approximately 8,500 psychiatrists in the nation in May, 1952, according to Dr. Daniel Blain, medical director of the American Psychiatric Association. Of these, about 3,500 devoted their full time to private practice, another 3,500 worked full time in mental hospitals, and the remainder divided their time between private practice and clinics, hospitals and other facilities.

We may expect more psychiatrists, for about 500 enter the field each year, although fifty retire, so the net gain is about 450. If this rate of increase is sustained, we shall have about 4,500 additional psychiatrists in another ten years, Dr. Blain estimates. Psychiatry is a fast growing medical specialty and one that attracts younger people—62 per cent are under forty-five.

Visits to a psychiatrist are usually made once a week. A troubled person may go only for one session or for several weeks, several months or a year, depending on his needs.

One man who lives in the suburbs of New York has traveled sixty miles every six months for the past twenty years to see his psychiatrist. The feeling of comfort he gets from this semi-annual visit sustains him the rest of the year. He visits his psychiatrist once every six months, just as others do their dentists.

There are inept psychiatrists, as there are inept men in all professions. Some, for instance, have not come far enough out of the mental hospital, where the accent is on diagnosis and custodial care. The broadening of psychiatry from diagnosis of the severely troubled to helping the less troubled calls for more skill on the part of the psychiatrist. No longer is it enough that he be able to give medication or reel off diagnostic terms.

"Diagnosis is a science; treatment partakes of this science but is itself essentially an art," explained one psychiatrist.

Some may know all the terminology but they cannot help the troubled feel better because they do not know the "art" of help.

A much-publicized Park Avenue psychiatrist falls into this category. One woman left his office in disgust.

"He spent the whole hour telling me how good he was," she said. "He didn't ask any questions about me. And I paid for that!"

Some psychiatrists help the troubled in schools and colleges. The young men who attend Yale University may be lucky for other reasons, but one reason is that, if they feel troubled, they have at hand the University Student Mental Hygiene Division. The present director, Dr. Clements C. Fry, joined it twenty-five years ago, and started helping troubled students at a time when the idea of psychiatry in a college met strong resistance. He is largely responsible for its developing into a valuable part of the university.

One student recently came for help because he was failing in his classes. He told the psychiatrist he did not understand why he could not study, because in high school he got some of the highest marks in class.

"Do you feel differently here than in high school?" asked the psychiatrist.

The boy paled, then said, "I hate it here."

"Why?" asked the psychiatrist.

"I can't seem to make any friends and I don't get along with the teachers," he said.

"Perhaps you're homesick," the psychiatrist said. "Many boys feel that way when they first leave home."

The young man took out a cigarette, relaxing for the first time since he entered the room. "I miss the family like hell," he said. "I feel like a child and I don't know what to do about it. I should be able to adjust to college life, but it seems I can't."

The psychiatrist asked him questions about his family. His mother and father had always made decisions for him, not realizing that when the time came for him to be on his own, he would feel lost. He had wanted to go to a midwestern college, but his father insisted on Yale.

"I feel bitter about that," he said.

"One college is pretty much like another—it's what you make of it," the psychiatrist assured him.

The young man visited the psychiatrist once a week. At the end of the semester he had passing marks. He made friends, among them several of his professors. The homesickness ebbed away.

The business world is starting to use the knowledge psychiatry has to offer. A group of Wall Street leaders made news when they met to discuss not the state of the nation's financial health but its emotional health.

Walter Maynard, president of the Association of Stock Exchange Firms, was host at the Harvard Club, New York, at a luncheon given in honor of Mental Health Week, 1952, and also in honor of Dr. Robert Knight, medical director of the Austen Riggs Center, Stockbridge, Massachusetts, internationally known for its study, research and treatment of psychoneurosis.

"As a result of both personal observation and considerable study at the layman's level, I know there is a greater opportunity for doing good in the general field of psychiatry than in any other branch of medicine or charity or, for that matter, politics," Mr. Maynard told his guests.

Business and industry "take a terrific beating" financially every year because they do not use available psychiatric knowledge or support psychiatric research, Dr. Knight said.

This applies not only to the loss of time of executives and employees because of emotional disturbances but to labor difficulties due to the lack of understanding of the fundamental principles of group psychology, he said.

It is heartening that a few large corporations, including the International Harvester Company and the General American Transportation Company, are starting to give money for research in psychiatry.

Settlement houses and youth clubs are asking psychiatrists to help their staff become more sensitive to the needs of children. For instance, Dr. Alexander Reid Martin, consulting psychiatrist to the Children's Aid Society in New York, helped draw up a questionnaire to find out what might be troubling some of the children at the seven centers maintained by the society.

One twelve-year-old girl showed by her answers that she was struggling against many fears inside herself:

Q: What do you like to play best in the whole club?

A: I don't know.

Q: Are you a good dancer?

A: No! No! Please.

Q: Do you like school?

A: No! Who likes school that comes here?

Q: What would you like to be when you grow up?

A: Well . . . I want to be a cowgirl.

Q: What does your mother want you to be when you grow up?

A: She doesn't tell me.

Q: What does your father want you to be?

A: I don't ask him.

Q: Do you play with your mother?

A: Fool around.

Q: Do you play with your father?

A: Yeah.

Q: If you had three wishes, what would you most wish for?

A: You mean things? A bike. Roller skates.

In discussing this girl with the staff, Dr. Martin asked what possible problems in her life might be indicated by her answers. Some of the staff comments were:

"This girl has fingerprints. But they are her only substantial identification. All else is lost within her family kingdom. No love, care or affection is shown her at home. Her mother has seven other children and spares little time for her."

"This unhappy child is groping and clawing for something to latch onto in order to avoid being completely swallowed up. She doesn't accept being a girl. She wants to be a cowgirl. She is horrified by the idea of dancing."

"She feels alone. She feels nobody cares about her so why should she care about herself?"

Settlement houses, traditionally concerned with the health of the neighboring community, seem a natural place to offer help to the troubled in the large cities. Several in New York, including Henry Street, Hudson Guild, Madison House and University Settlement, operate state-licensed psychiatric clinics for those who live nearby.

Psychiatry has just started to penetrate prison walls. One of those who has long recognized the importance of giving men and women who commit crimes an understanding of why they broke the law is Henrietta Additon, superintendent of New York State's only prison for women, Westfield State Farm.

Her struggle to get help for the prisoners was rewarded when the state finally allocated funds for a part-time psychiatrist. Dr. Ruth Glueck Addison, daughter of Dr. Bernard Glueck, psychiatrist, leads group therapy classes, helps some of the women individually, and works with the staff so they may know why some troubled people rebel against society.

A number of the prisoners are not bashful about asking for help, Dr. Addison has found. "People pay a lot of money for this outside," one woman was overheard to remark to another.

A feeling shared by many women who land in prison is

that their parents expected them to be "bad," Dr. Addison noted. "These girls have grown up with the immutable belief they *are* bad—just as though they were born with one leg," she commented. "It is as if they are here because they wanted to punish their parents for making them feel bad and, at the same time, carry out the prediction of their parents."

Dr. Miriam Van Waters, superintendent of the Massachusetts Reformatory for Women at Framingham, Massachusetts, is another of the nation's leaders in bringing psychiatry to a prison, not for diagnosis but treatment. Because of her understanding, this reformatory possesses an atmosphere of hope rather than punishment.

Psychiatrists are found in courts, providing help for the troubled and aiding judges to understand how crime and delinquency are rooted in fear. They also lend moral support to the underpaid, overworked men and women of our probation and parole departments who are giving much unheralded help.

There are few groups today that do not use psychiatrists or psychiatric concepts. Recently the missionaries started taking to psychiatry. They are considering such questions, according to a recent release from the Missions Public Relations Office, as:

"How to establish a line between self-sacrifice and pathological self-sacrifice?"

"How to establish an attitude toward sex which is neither prudery nor sentimentality?"

The psychiatric clinic is a new and fast-developing institution. A complete list of all the psychiatric clinics of the nation, state by state, is contained in a 138-page directory that may be obtained from the National Association of Mental Health, 1790 Broadway, for $1.25, or from the individual state mental hygiene societies. It includes: community psychiatric clinics (name, address and auspices); mental health associations (state and local); state institutions for the mentally ill, the mentally deficient and epileptics; state governmental mental health facilities and hospitals, and psychiatric hospitals and facilities, and hospitals operated by the Veterans Administration and other federal agencies.

Among those operating clinics throughout the country are general hospitals, social agencies, psychiatric institutes, mental hospitals, states, cities, towns, colleges, high schools, settlement houses and independent groups of psychiatrists or psychoanalysts. Some clinics offer free services; others charge whatever the troubled person can afford.

Clinics have started in various ways. For instance, while in the Navy as medical officers, two psychiatrists, Dr. Edward D. Hoedemaker and Dr. Douglas W. Orr, decided that a private clinic offering psychiatric care would meet a need in the Northwest. When they got out of the Navy, they found a large, comfortable building on a quiet street in Seattle and started the Northwest Clinic of Psychiatry and Neurology.

It isn't only the Kentucky Derby for which Louisville is noted today. Dr. Spafford Ackerly and his group have made Louisville famous for helping the troubled. They planned and arranged for the staffing of community clinics for children and adults, helped by psychiatrists, psychiatric social workers and mental health nurses. The community responded by raising funds to erect a model wing for the treatment of psychiatric patients in the Norton Memorial Infirmary in Louisville.

We do not have enough clinics to meet our need, but that is because of the shortage of psychiatrists to staff them.

There is a scarcity among all groups that help the troubled. A recent bulletin published by the National Mental Health Institute, an agency of the U. S. Public Health Service, carried advertisements for a psychiatrist to develop a mental care program in Alaska, for a psychiatrist familiar with child guidance work to join the Bureau of Mental Hygiene in Hawaii, for a clinical psychologist in Arizona, for a psychiatric social worker in Iowa to act as a consultant to six mental health centers, and for a psychiatric social worker to help organize the mental health and youth conservation programs in Minnesota.

But notwithstanding the shortage, help is available to those who need it and are persistent about getting it, even though they may have to wait.

CHAPTER 8

Psychoanalysis—"Sleeping Memories of the Past"

THE deepest form of help available to the troubled is psychoanalysis.

The nature of psychoanalysis is misunderstood by many. Some think of it as a mixture of magic and witchcraft. Some believe it sheer nonsense. Others speak of it with such anger as might shake the stars.

What is psychoanalysis? When Dr. Joseph Miller, medical director of Hillside Hospital, Long Island, N. Y., finished his analysis, he recalls that his analyst, the late Dr. Franz Wittels, asked: "Well, what have you learned?"

"I had learned 550,000 things, as you do in analysis," says Dr. Miller, "but I was so overcome by the question that all I could think of at the moment was that I had stopped biting my nails. So I said to Dr. Wittels, 'I've stopped biting my nails.' "

Dr. Wittels looked at him with a sick expression and said, "Expensive manicure, wasn't it?"

What is "learned" in analysis, if anything is "learned," is the self. As you come to know the self, you discover you have repeated the same vain attempts to solve the same superficial problems over the years, never coming to terms with the real trouble. You could not know the deeper problems, because they were hidden in the unconscious.

"Our arms and legs are full of sleeping memories of the past," wrote Proust. In analysis, you reach for those sleeping memories of the arms and legs by talking about yourself.

Talk is the tool of analysis, which those not in analysis sometimes find difficult to understand. Freud declared: "The patient's unenlightened relatives—people of a kind to be impressed only by something visible and tangible, preferably by the sort of 'action' that may be seen at a cinema—never omit to express their doubts of how 'mere talk can possibly cure anybody.' Their reasoning is, of course, as illogical as it is inconsistent. For they are the same people who are always convinced that the sufferings of neurotics are purely 'in their own imagination.' "

He says of words: "Words and magic were in the beginning one and the same thing, and even today words retain much of their magical power. By words one of us can give to another the greatest happiness or bring about utter despair; by words the teacher imparts his knowledge to the student; by words the orator sweeps his audience with him and determines its judgments and decisions. Words call forth emotions and are universally the means by which we influence our fellow-creatures. Therefore, let us not despise the use of words in psychotherapy."

Psychoanalysis is words, but it is more than words. Men have been talking over their troubles with each other since the first two came upon the earth. Sometimes it helped, but more often it did not. The answer to why it did not help is the answer to why psychoanalysis does.

At first, Freud, like some others since, thought that after the analyst had discovered the troubled person's motives, he could tell him what they were and he would be cured, says Dr. Ives Hendrick, psychoanalyst. Freud would learn the unconscious motive, tell the patient, the patient would say he understood, but nothing happened.

Freud learned a lesson "which many who putter with his technique have not yet assimilated," says Dr. Hendrick—that "intellectual insight cannot control the forces of the unconscious, that repression is not simply the difference between knowing and not knowing, that cure depends on far more than making conscious."

Understanding why we behave as we do will not make us feel less troubled. We may intellectualize until doomsday but be no happier. Deep change occurs only when intellectual understanding is accompanied by a release of the emotion that caused the feelings to be buried in the unconscious in the first place. This emotion can be expressed only when you feel someone cares enough about you that he will like you in spite of all your faults and weaknesses. You then become free enough to talk in a different way.

In ordinary conversation, we speak of what we know consciously. Even when we are discussing our problems with a friend or a minister, we talk as logically and straightforwardly as we are able. We tell what we believe we know about our past. If we can be helped by their advice and comfort, all to the good. But sometimes this is not enough.

Psychoanalysis offers a special kind of talk which leads to the hidden sources of trouble. Because of the trust you develop in the analyst, you discuss feelings and thoughts you would hesitate to admit to a friend or family doctor, who, no matter how sympathetic, cannot give the disciplined love necessary to help.

The analyst looks at you objectively. He is not involved with you personally, as a friend might be. He is a doctor, and you accept him as such, knowing his task is to help you feel better. You lie on a couch, a relaxed position that permits your thoughts to flow more freely. He sits at the head of the couch, out of sight.

He encourages you to talk in a new way. You do not sift and consider your thoughts, organizing them as you would in everyday living. You let them drift, one idea suggesting the next. You say whatever comes to mind, whether sense or nonsense, whether related to your life today or childhood. You talk of dreams and daydreams. You see yourself as a baby, a child, an adolescent. You tell what frightened you, what pleased you, what you longed for, what disgusted you. This is called "free association" and its purpose is to reveal the hidden self to the conscious self.

One woman's associations ran as follows:

"I went shopping yesterday for a party dress—I couldn't find what I wanted—what did I want?—I wanted a dark blue dress like the first party dress I ever had—it was dark blue, white collar—it fitted tight around the bodice—I remember feeling the tightness—my first party dress—my first feeling of growing up—my breasts stuck out—I think I was a bit ashamed —other girls didn't seem to have such big breasts—"

This woman had repressed many feelings about her femininity. One of the dilemmas of the troubled may be mixed feelings about their role as a man or woman. They feel, somehow, that if they had been born the opposite sex their parents would have loved them.

"My mother hated little boys," one man told an analyst.

"So in your child-mind, the only other thing you could be, to win her love, was a little girl," said the analyst gently. "And over the years you have kept from yourself that struggle."

The hidden part of the mind is constantly trying to break through into consciousness and express itself. But it does not do this directly. Its messages arrive in disguised, subtle form. Psychoanalysis helps clarify the messages sent by the unconscious.

The troubled cannot reach their unconscious alone. For, the unconscious is "utterly unknown and cannot be voluntarily recalled," as the late Dr. A. A. Brill, one of the country's pioneer psychoanalysts, put it.

Why cannot the troubled help themselves to know themselves? Because they are their own worst enemy. The self-hatred which they possess interferes with knowledge of self and to them "the obvious is not the obvious," as Dr. Victor Eisenstein, psychoanalyst, puts it.

"Self-analysis doesn't work because the counter-transference is too hostile," said one analyst, speaking the truth sometimes contained in jest.

"Transference" is the term used to describe your feelings toward the analyst. "Counter-transference" applies to his feelings toward you. Combined, they add up to the heart of analysis.

You transfer to the analyst the way you have felt about the important people in your life—your mother, father, brother or sister. Once again you live through childhood fear, rage, desire, frustration—impossible by yourself, but possible when someone encourages you to face yourself.

But that person must be someone who is able to help you break through the defenses you have built as protection against the dangers which you felt threatened you with death as a child. You do not give up protection easily, for you are not sure you will live if you relinquish what you feel has saved your life thus far.

Anything that exists may be used as a defense—work, sex, success, illness, food, glamor, intellect, reading.

One woman spent years reading all the books she could acquire on psychology. She admitted, "I couldn't find in my library the answers to what was bothering me."

"You'll find them only in the library of yourself," said the analyst.

"But I don't understand the language in which *those* books are written," she replied, referring to the unconscious.

"Only because it's still unfamiliar to you," he said. "Keep using it and you will understand."

Our defenses are actually weakness, for they keep us from understanding ourselves. The psychic medicine we dole out to ourselves is more harmful than the psychic sickness. Compromises do not work, for there is no compromise with truth.

We cannot get through the defenses to our inner self by reading poetry, philosophy or fiction. We may feel better for the moment if we see a movie which makes us weep or take a drink which relaxes us. But we do not come to grips with what is causing torment either by sharing someone else's experiences or blotting out our own. Identifying with someone is not the same as discovering the self. It may be used to avoid the sterner task of facing the self.

Freud wrote to his friend, Wilhelm Fleiss, that "true self-analysis is impossible." He added, "The forces opposing themselves are too strong." Yet Freud had to try self-analysis, for at the time no other analyst existed. He tells about it in a group of letters to Fleiss, excerpts of which were read for the first time in this country at a meeting of the American Psychoanalytic Association, by Dr. Martin Grotjahn, who translated some of them.

Freud wrote to Dr. Fleiss, a Berlin physician whom Dr. Grotjahn described as Freud's "analyst-by-correspondence": "I can analyze myself only with what I have understood in others."

By looking deep into himself, he discovered the meaning of dreams and the role of repression. His self-analysis reinforced his theory of the importance of the Oedipus complex.

"The main patient who keeps me busy am I myself," he wrote in one letter. "The analysis is more difficult than any other one. This is the reason which paralyzes my psychic power for description and report about the former gains. I believe, however, that it has to be done and that it is a necessary connecting link in my work."

Another passage contained the first discovery in himself of incest. It read: "My self-analysis is indeed the most important thing I have going on right now, and it promises to become of the highest value for me if it can be carried through to an end . . .

"To be completely honest with oneself is good training. Only one single thought of general value came to me. I have found in myself the infatuation with the mother and the jealousy towards the father, and I consider it now as a usual event of early childhood.

"If that is so, then the gripping power of King Oedipus becomes understandable in spite of all objections which the intelligence raises against the acceptance of Fatum. The Greek mythology contains an inner urge which everybody recognizes because it leads back to one's own inner feelings.

Every one of the listeners to the great drama has been such an Oedipus, which one recognizes when one shudders at the thought of the crime and its presentation in the drama."

In another paragraph of this letter, as Dr. Grotjahn points out, Freud wrote "the simple striking sentence":

"Hamlet's conscience is his unconscious guilt feelings."

How true it is that our unconscious guilt feelings make cowards of us all.

Freud did the best he could to analyze himself. But there is evidence the analysis was primarily intellectual and that, as some of his later letters show, he remained unhappy all his life. He could not feel substantially happier, according to some authorities, because he did not absorb from another person the quality of safety necessary for the emotional acceptance of self.

Another must care about you before you can care about yourself. The feeling that he cared about them is what Freud gave his patients and what analysts today give their patients, perhaps in even greater degree. This belief that someone cares about you enables you to look into yourself.

"Why am I troubled?" a man demanded of an analyst.

"Because of everything in your life," the analyst replied. "You must search and research to find out why. I can give you no pat, patronizing answer. You must explore the whole."

Sometimes you find out that truth is the opposite of what you have believed over the years.

A woman insisted she adored her mother. Then one day she blurted out defiantly, "When my mother would bandage my cuts, I would rip off the bandages! I didn't want her hands touching me. I wanted the sun and the air to cleanse my wounds."

"I thought you said you adored her," remarked the analyst.

"I'd live in spite of her—I'd live to spite her!" stormed the woman. "I'd show her she couldn't boss me."

The "adoration" assumed when she was a little girl masked deep fear and hatred of a tyrannical mother who allowed her little freedom of thought or deed.

Some know they hate parents, and have no difficulty confessing it. In analysis, as you grow to like yourself, you accept and like your parents, realizing they are human beings and not the gods or devils they may have seemed over the years. You feel more a part of parents, yet apart from them.

As one man said: "Analysis helped me face the reality of my childhood and accept my parents as human; disturbed, yes—but two who did the best they could."

Everyone does the best he can although on the surface it may appear differently. One mother abandoned her three-year-old son on a lonely road.

"How could she do such a cruel, vicious thing?" stormed the man who found the child and brought him to the nearest police station.

"She might have done something worse," remarked a thoughtful police officer.

"What could be worse?" asked the man angrily.

"She might have killed him. Some mothers do," said the police officer calmly.

This was a parent for whom the lesser of two evils was to get rid of her child before she harmed him. She was unconsciously protecting her life and the child's as best she could in view of the depth of her fear and anger.

Our unconscious gets through to us in several ways the feelings and thoughts we have banished to our psychic limbo. The limbo will contain only so many of them only so long and then, if overburdened, or if a crisis in our life weakens our defenses, it will start shooting back what we have forgotten in disguised form.

Slips of the tongue, for instance, indicate what we know unconsciously but not consciously.

"I'll see you when I get back from Buffalo," one man told his wife.

She looked at him in surprise. "I thought you were going to Chicago," she said.

"I am," he corrected himself. "I didn't mean Buffalo."

He thought about this during his analytic session. "Why did I say Buffalo?" he mused. "Buffalo—let me see. I had an aunt who lived in Buffalo whom I loved as a child. I always looked forward to visiting her. Buffalo was a place I wanted to go. I detest Chicago. Chicago means long hours with business acquaintances—hard work."

Dreams also reveal our unconscious to us. Freud called dreams "the royal road to the unconscious, representing the hidden fulfillment of an unconscious wish." Which led a layman, Bennett Epstein, to comment, "Psychoanalysis is the new science built on the rough stuff of dreams."

Of those who say they know nothing about what they dream, Freud remarked, "I assure you that it is not only quite possible, but highly probable, that the dreamer really does know the meaning of his dream; *only he does not know that he knows, and therefore thinks that he does not.*" (Italics are Freud's.)

Erich Fromm, lay analyst, has compared an unanalyzed dream to "an unopened letter to the self."

Many elements of dreams are symbolic. Water, for example, may stand for childbirth because of the association of amniotic fluid with the birth of a baby. Freud and other analysts have found there is a general tendency to dream in symbols and that the symbols may be shared in common. Thus the analyst has shortcuts available to help one understand the meaning of a dream.

Dreams open up the torment of taboos. The physical yearning for a parent, for instance, may forever hold one unconscious captive unless, unlike Hamlet, he faces what lies in his dreams.

A temperate amount of incestuous feeling is natural, for in that way we become attracted to the opposite sex. But if we live in fear, the incestuous feelings, as all else in life, are overstimulated beyond the natural state and become so terrifying they must be hidden from consciousness.

In analysis, sexuality applies to all of one's bodily feelings from infancy on, of which sexual intercourse is only a part. It includes toilet functions, eating habits and how we feel about persons of our own sex, among other things.

Dreams may show that a deep chasm exists between "sex" and "love." Because some are so afraid of their bodies, they must put sex and love in separate categories. They dare not think of sex as part of love, dare not believe they are entitled to enjoy sex with someone towards whom they feel tender.

For some the defense against fear is the denying of sex, which is a negation of self.

For others, excessive use of sex becomes a defense. They live as if sex were all, plunging their whole life's sensations into it. It is as though there were nothing before and would be nothing after, as if the one moment were worth the whole of living. Sex possesses them; they do not possess themselves.

"The touch of flesh seems to be your only friend, but it is a false one," one analyst told a young man who had many affairs. "When you live for sex, it is as though you are putting your life in someone else's hands."

Those who must seduce do not seduce out of love, but to ease troubled feelings. Seduction, like alcohol, is no answer to fear. Fear must be faced in order to be dissolved.

"You have been afraid to hold someone's hand or look into their eyes, but must head straight for that part of the body which you feel is most easily thrown away," one analyst told a man who had gone from one woman to the next. "Life is not ecstasy or nothing. There's a lot in between, like the holding of a hand."

When sex is such a desperate need, it holds in it danger and violence. It is not a tender, passionate act with meaning but a deed of fury and forgetfulness. It is used as a release of frustration, not as a way to pleasure.

The man who insists his buttocks be burned with a hot iron as he indulges in the sexual act, the men who must whip women and the women who must be whipped (and vice versa) show the extreme in the need for violence. A lesser degree of this feeling exists in some of the troubled who must punish themselves and others for what they believe shameful and wicked. Their parents have made them feel they would be cursed beyond the wildest ravings should they succumb to the strong desires that flame inside them.

At first Freud strongly emphasized the deep trouble caused by the repression of sexual feelings. Later in his career he began to inquire into life and death forces, and how man fights to survive as well as to procreate.

Those who think that the quality and quantity of fear in a life determines how troubled a man is, believe that he is ruled by a life force which contains both the need to survive and to procreate. The two needs are so interwoven they cannot be separated.

Sexual feelings are the "core" of the life force and are deeply affected by a man's need to save his life when he feels it threatened, but repression of sex is not the primary cause of troubled feelings, they maintain.

If one has lived in psychological terror as a child, many things in his life (including the need to express sexual feelings) will not function normally and may over-work or under-work as he fights what he feels may be death with all the resources he possesses.

Analysis enables you to discover you have acted first in self-preservation. You did what you had to do in order to keep alive. There was no "right" or "wrong" to it. It was a matter of sheer survival.

It is natural for each man to want to save his life. Those who try to offer their lives as a kind of sacrifice to others, giving up all their own rights and desires, only stir up more un-happiness. Secretly, they are trying to save their own lives. They believe unconsciously that only by self-sacrifice can they deserve to live. But their actions usually create only resent-ment and anger in others.

If there is desperate fight for survival in a man, his psy-chic pain will be intense. He will need the deep help offered by psychoanalysis.

One hears the complaint that psychoanalysis is expensive. It is expensive if one looks at the immediate price, but it may be extremely cheap in view of the suffering it eases. Such suffering cannot be measured in dollars.

The relief of intense, complicated pain, whether physical or emotional, costs money because it requires so much skill, understanding and time on the part of the one who heals.

Analysts are few. There are 520 members in the American Psychoanalytic Association—although not all analysts belong to this group—and 1,000 more are in training. Their prepara-tion is highly expensive. They not only go through the long course required of the ordinary physician, but add to it years of study of emotional behavior, plus their own psychoanaly-sis, called a training analysis. This takes money and what Freud called "a long and severe discipline and training in self-control."

There are also lay analysts. They do not have a medical degree but they have been analyzed and have intensively studied emotional problems. Most of them have a degree in psychology. They are few in comparison with the analysts who have a medical degree, but their number is growing.

When any service is scarce, we must expect to pay a steep price for it. As more analysts are trained, the price of analysis may drop.

One reason analysis seems costly is that the troubled have difficulty believing they are worth anything, let alone $15 an hour. They will give thousands of dollars for new furniture or a trip to Europe but will not dream of spending such a large sum on themselves and their eventual happiness. Once in analysis, though, they accept their worth more easily.

Today's prices range from $10 to $25 a visit, with the average around $15. Most of the nation's analysts live in the large cities, principally New York, Boston, Chicago, Los Angeles.

A woman wrote from a small town in Iowa asking, "What can I do about getting to an analyst?" The only answer was, "Move to Chicago." There was not a single analyst in the state of Iowa.

There are only a few analysts in Faulkner territory. Southern psychological history was made recently when one analyst and three others in training settled in Chapel Hill, North Carolina. There is a growing number of analysts in all the larger cities—north, east, south and west.

In comparison with the other groups that give help, psychoanalysts are small in number. But the impact of analysis is felt far beyond those who receive this kind of help.

Psychoanalysis is changing medicine, the law, education, welfare. Its theories are permeating all the professions that help the troubled. They are reaching ministers, doctors, teachers, judges, nurses, lawyers and policemen, as well as social workers and psychiatrists.

Psychoanalysis is becoming an integral part of the psychological profession which at one point ignored it. G. Stanley Hall, president of Clark University, in 1920, wrote in the preface to the American edition of Freud's *A General Introduction to Psychoanalysis*:

". . . Freudian themes have rarely found a place on the program of the American Psychological Association."

He should have seen the 1952 program! There were still papers devoted to such topics as:

"Anxiety and Conditioning in Salt Water Fishes"

"An Experimental Study of the Color Vision of the Giant Tortoise"

"An Investigation of Learning in the Earthworm"

"Investigations of the Behavior of the Paramecium Aurelia"

But there were major papers on such subjects as:

"Two Levels of Unconscious Awareness"

"The Personalities of Successful and Less Successful Psychotherapists"

"A Comparison of the Psychological Environments Two Communities Provide for Children"

"The Mental Patient Looks at 'Snake Pit'"

An increasing number of psychologists and social workers are being analyzed so they may give help with a deeper understanding of the power of the unconscious.

Psychoanalysis is widening many frontiers. It has shown, for instance, that a number of those believed mentally retarded are actually emotionally ill. They are so afraid of and furious at their parents that they refuse to think. Once given psychoanalytic help, some start to care enough about themselves to use their minds.

Psychoanalysis has also given rise to group therapy. This is a form of help in which several troubled persons get together and talk about common problems. Group therapy classes may be led by a psychoanalyst or by a psychologist with psychoanalytic training.

In one group therapy class for mothers sponsored by a family agency, a psychologist acts as leader, helping the women understand themselves. At one session their conversation, in part, went as follows:

First mother (sighing): I had the same trouble with Johnny last night. He wouldn't go to bed. First I asked him nicely, then I asked him not so nicely, and then, as usual, I had to slap him.

Second mother: Did you *have* to?

First mother: I hate myself for doing it, but I can't seem to get him to behave any other way.

Third mother: Have you tried just talking to him quietly?

First mother: He won't listen.

Fourth mother: Losing your temper and slapping him doesn't help either of you.

First mother (losing her temper slightly): You should have that kid for two hours!

Psychologist (gently): Have you tried to put yourself in Johnny's place? To understand why he might not want to go to bed?

First mother: I don't have the time to think about those things.

Third mother: If you take the time, you'll find you won't have to lose your temper, maybe.

Fifth mother: I'd exchange my daughter for Johnny. Yesterday she comes right out and asks me to tell her the facts of life. At the age of ten!

Third mother: Didn't you want to know them when you were ten?

Fifth mother (surprised): Why, I guess I did.

Sixth mother (shyly): I remember asking *my* mother questions. I felt so afraid. She didn't help me, either. She just warned me to stay away from boys.

Third mother: If my mother had handled me differently, I'd be able to feel freer with my children.

Psychologist: But you're a person in your own right. You don't have to do things the way your mother did. You are not your mother.

Third mother: It's taking me a long time to separate myself from her.

The federal government is sponsoring modified group analysis for some of its top executives. "Seminars in Human Relations" are conducted by Dr. Henry P. Laughlin, psychoanalyst, who is president of the Washington Psychiatric Society, to help "good executives become better."

During a recent session, the men noticed that one member seemed unusually quiet and withdrawn.

"What's the matter, Tom?" asked one of them.

Tom's lips quivered. He said in a choked voice, "I don't feel so well today."

"Any special reason?" asked another. "Did you have a bad dream last night?"

Everyone laughed except Tom.

"I'm sorry, boys," he said. "I'm a wet blanket today."

"Maybe we can help you," said the man next to him. "Let us in on it."

Tom drew a deep breath. Then he said, "It's just that my mother died last night."

There was silence. Each man in the room knew what that meant—to himself and to Tom.

One of them got up from his chair, put his arm across Tom's shoulders. Another said softly, "No wonder you're upset."

Tom looked at them gratefully. "I didn't mean to say anything about it," he apologized.

"That would have been unrealistic," said one of the men. "This is one of the deepest tragedies to strike anyone. We're all with you, old man."

By sharing his feelings with the group and getting their sympathy and support, it was easier for Tom to bear his loss. Helped during his own emotional crisis, he could understand how others might wish to be helped during theirs.

The executives have found the study of their own emotions valuable. One said, "I feel I have received a lot of help and this has been reflected in my work."

Another commented, "The practice of examining my own motivation has helped me to be more tolerant and accepting of the behavior of others with whom I work, whereas formerly I might have been impatient, scornful, or authoritative in the same situation."

A third declared, "Many times I was able to see that self-interest had been more governing in my behavior than I first appreciated, and that, perhaps, I was not being as considerate as I could be of the self-interests of the other folks."

Group therapy is also being used with the severely troubled in mental hospitals, prisoners, narcotic addicts, alcoholics, troubled children.

Experience in a group gives a chance at self-exploration to some who otherwise might not accept help. Perhaps they need no deeper help than the group offers. A number undertake individual analysis as a result of starting to know themselves in a group. Some receive both individual help and group therapy.

Group therapy may vary in depth. Some groups discuss problems on a superficial basis. Others endeavor to probe the unconscious, bringing up dreams and subjects considered taboo.

What takes place in the group is believed to be basically the same as in individual help, although compared with psychoanalysis it is "a more superficial type of treatment," explains Saul Scheidlinger, clinical psychologist and group therapy consultant. Deeply repressed unconscious conflicts are "rarely reached" through the group approach alone, he says.

For those who truly want to look into themselves, psychoanalysis is the only answer. An increasing number of the troubled who want to throw off the fear that has plagued them all their lives are entering psychoanalysis. They realize the unhappiness of the past haunts the present and future. They want to understand the past so the future may be happier.

Perhaps some symptom has signalled them that all is not well—insomnia, persistent headaches, depressions, uneasiness. More people are realizing that when the smooth flow of living is broken, nature is warning them something is wrong.

A man who attended a party in New York found himself the only one in a room of fifteen persons who was not being analyzed. "Everyone was talking about *his* analyst," he said bitterly. "I felt like an orphan."

The owner of a large advertising firm remarked, "When a new employee starts, I ask what time he goes to the analyst and whether our business hours will interfere."

And the managing editor of a publishing house, noting how many of his staff were being analyzed, suggested ironically, "Wouldn't it be easier if we simply hired a staff psychoanalyst?"

One man who had just started analysis was finding the going difficult. But he insisted he would stick it out. "Quit?" he roared. "Why, that would be like passing up the big show."

But analysis is not "the big show." The one who embarks on it is not a spectator. He is a participant in a relationship deeper than any other he has known except with his parents. Out of it comes the chance to know the self.

CHAPTER 9

Can Human Nature Change?

THROUGH the centuries the rationalization, "You can't change human nature," has been used to exploit people emotionally. Whenever the status quo suits someone's selfish needs, this old saw is trotted out.

Psychoanalysis shows that human nature can change. It brings about what some analysts have called "the internal change which leads to the mastery of the self."

Psychoanalysis is a look inward for the purpose of change.

[121]

Change comes as the self is accepted. Then one also accepts others, rather than tolerating them, as one has previously tolerated the self.

But this kind of change takes time. One must grow up again, in an emotional sense. If we could find out how to shorten days and years, we might then shorten the period of analysis. But as yet, no scientist has come through with a way to speed the growth of a child.

The familiar feel of trouble has advantages that are difficult to let go. Not in vain did Dryden write:

> There is a pleasure sure
> In being mad which none but madmen know.

But this is a deceptive pleasure, part of the deeper pain. Unhappiness is caused by what is believed to be the way of pleasure out of pain, but this easy way only adds to torment.

We give up troubled feelings only as we come to know that the more painful way of life is *not* to give them up. Nothing else will convince us of the error of our feelings.

Analysis reduces panic and desperation, but until you become stronger you do not move out of the pattern of your life. The unconscious takes a lot of jolting before it helps set you free. In the meantime, you may stall against giving up what you believe are advantages, wasting many an hour, day, or week, by not talking or talking about things that do not matter.

The hard part of the fight against feeling troubled is *wanting* to wage it. It is easy to give in to troubled feelings. The turning point comes when one decides to "will." This does not happen at any one time but slowly and gradually, as all else happens in analysis. It occurs as trust in the analyst and then in the self grows deeper.

The trust that develops in analysis sinks in slowly like the warm sun. If you get a strong dose of sunburn all at once, you are apt to suffer pain, blister, lose your skin and wind up with no tan. But if you absorb sun in easy doses, day by day, you acquire a deep, lasting tan. So it goes with trust.

In a way, the analyst becomes the good parent who makes possible self-love and self-respect. The feel of love, unfamiliar to the troubled, is not accepted overnight. Deep emotional wounds cannot be forgotten quickly.

Some have difficulty understanding the need for time. One woman walked into the office of a New York analyst, sat herself down and announced, "I've come from Cleveland to be analyzed."

"It may take quite a while," the analyst told her.

"Oh, I've arranged to be here for the week," she said blithely.

Psychoanalysis is not a game to be played for a week or so. It is a difficult, sometimes painful process, taking time, money, energy and thought. To paraphrase Shakespeare, "There are more things 'twixt the conscious and unconscious, Horatio, than are dreamt of in your philosophy."

The goal of analysis is to know the self, accept the self, and then change that about the self which has caused unhappiness.

The troubled cannot accept themselves in a few, miraculous sessions. The real suffering, the things of which men dare not speak unless they know each other well, may take many a full moon to reach.

We do not give up suffering easily, for suffering has become an ally. We have chosen it as the lesser of two evils. We have preferred to suffer rather than die of shame or violence. We have accepted one kind of suffering as pledge against what we feel must be a worse one.

It is difficult to talk of suffering but talk we must if we are to ease pain. Many live choked by unspoken suffering. They possess words enough but they use the words to cover up truth. They do not speak of what gnaws at their vitals.

Only after a year of analysis was one woman able to speak of a childhood incident which had embarrassed her. She described how, one night when she was sleeping in the same bed with her brother, she reached out and explored his body.

"I never said a word about this to anyone before," she sobbed. "Over the years I have wanted to tell him how sorry I was. I felt ashamed and guilty, as if I had violated him. This feeling of shame still hangs suspended between us each time I see him."

She had lived with this suffering, sharing it with no one by a word, although her life was full of thousands of other words.

"I thought it was such a little thing," she said, drying her tears.

"Perhaps you had to fill your life with many other things to make it seem little," suggested the analyst.

"All I know is that I have terrible guilt," she said.

"Didn't it occur to you that most children explore each other's bodies?" he asked.

"No," she replied.

"Why didn't it?"

"I felt too horror-stricken to think," she said. *"Do* most children?"

"If they're not too frightened," he said. "It's part of their natural curiosity."

Her natural curiosity had been thwarted, covered by layers of unnatural guilt. Her spirit of adventure had been frozen by the tyranny of fear.

When you do not face the real suffering, you live in fantasy to ease the pain. Reality is what most people observe, the world as it is. Fantasy is a private world moulded to your needs, existing only in your imagination.

Fantasy produces pain of a subtle, devious, destructive nature. The pain of reality is psychic peanuts compared to the agony fantasy brings. Nature does not want us to escape the responsibility of reality; she exacts a stiff toll from those who try.

One man who lived in extreme fantasy thought everyone was trying to poison him. His life was a veritable hell. He felt there was no escape from death because no one loved him, everyone wished him dead.

Those who rush through life without drinking in or digesting its meaning are living in fantasy to a lesser degree. They will not stop to see what the world is like. They want only to escape from reality and from themselves.

"I feel as though I am always zooming along in a car at

eighty miles an hour, never knowing whether I will crash over a precipice or skid around a dangerous curve into another car," one troubled man confessed.

"You should slow up, drive along at forty miles an hour, enjoying the scenery of life, and give up the mad exhilaration of a crazy existence," said the analyst.

"Why do I run so fast?"

"You are trying to run away from yourself. You are not accepting what is real. You live in a world of fantasy."

Fantasy is hard to fight because you do not know what you fight. It is as though you were running down a dark street, shooting a gun wildly or swinging a knife blindly. The enemy is unseen.

Some live so completely in fantasy their feet scarcely ever touch the ground of reality. They lose the rewards and joys of life we all deserve. They do not possess themselves. The unconscious possesses them.

It takes time to feel safe enough to know the unconscious. One man who had just started analysis said resentfully, "I feel impatient with the tediousness, the slowness, the lack of apparent progress. I wonder, too, just how in hell one gets at unconscious material. Can't it be done in some other, more efficient way?"

Not until we find a substitute for the love that leads to trust.

There is no trick to "getting at" the unconscious. It is not a thing apart from you. It flows along with the conscious and will come out as you feel freer. The impatience with lack of progress lessens as the analysis progresses, as anxiety, both conscious and unconscious, decreases.

As you make conscious the unconscious, you are more able to steer the course of your life. Events that once loomed as emergencies fall into proper perspective, and frustrations of daily living slowly fade away.

It takes time to accept that one is troubled, that one would not be unhappy unless something had gone wrong in childhood or infancy. Yet, until one can know that, suffering will continue, for the belief that one is happy when he is unhappy is self-deceit. Deceit hides but does not relieve suffering.

As children, the troubled absorbed from parents, or those with whom they lived, not what they wanted or willed but what was in the air. They sucked up fear as a sponge does water. They had no choice.

"I've always done what I wanted," one man insisted.

"You've been driven by your unconscious," replied the analyst. "You've acted on impulse, not conviction."

"Why have I no convictions?" the man demanded.

"Because you have not felt free enough to gain them. As a child you took as gospel what your parents handed out. You never thought for yourself."

Analysis reduces the fear in a life so one may have choice, so he is not buffeted by a past that hurls him wildly into the future.

It takes time to overcome the helplessness one felt as a child, to admit it and then decide to help oneself. Fortunately, once committed to safety, there is no other way. The emotional waves may kick up, but there's no turning back on the voyage into self.

It takes time to face and give up the self-pity which is part of troubled feelings. If some counted up the minutes a day spent in feeling sorry for themselves, they would be astounded at the staggering total. Self-pity is a protection hard to drop. Yet one must let go of it to feel better.

It takes time to combine erotic feelings and warm, tender love—not oppose them. Psychoanalysis does not encourage promiscuity, but maturity; part of maturity is the ability to settle down with one person for a lifetime, enjoying him or her sexually as well as other ways.

It takes time to give up the defenses that have served to protect from fear. There are two main types of defense—use of the mind (thought) or of bodily sensations (feeling). Those who resort to excessive thinking because they are afraid to feel, are detached, cool, unemotional. Those who resort to excessive feeling, fearing to think, live on impulse, blown hither and yon by the moment's whim.

Neither accepts himself. Both feel unloved and unwanted. Analysis encourages the expression of feeling in those who have been unable to feel, and thought in those who have been unable to think, so they are able to combine feeling and thought in balanced quantity and come up with reason.

It takes time to acquire a philosophy of life born of contemplation, if you lack one. Analysis may involve obtaining new values that are workable and real, if you have none or if the ones you possess are distorted.

One man, who gave up analysis because he said he did

not think it was worth the trouble (it was getting more difficult for him to face himself) told the analyst, "If it's a question of spending more money on analysis or a new automobile, I'm choosing the automobile."

"Where are your values?" asked the analyst gently.

"I didn't come here to discuss values—I came for help,"
retorted the man.

The two cannot be separated. Unless the troubled person
acquires some sort of philosophy, he will toss around like a
boat without a rudder. An analyst "should possess the ability
to work out with the patient a philosophy the patient can
use," says Dr. Nolan D. C. Lewis, director of the New York
State Psychiatric Institute.

"I never read Shakespeare or the Bible until I was analyzed," confessed one man. "I didn't care about a philosophi-
cal approach to life. I was too intent on beating myself up
psychologically."

Some gain religious faith during analysis. Religion and
psychoanalysis are not in opposition. They are "complemen-
tary," as the Rev. James Van der Veldt, professor of psychology and psychiatry at the Catholic University of America,
once said.

In the past few years religion and psychoanalysis have
joined hands. Prominent religious leaders of all denomina-
tions write and speak of the cooperative part they play. The
magazine, *Pastoral Psychology*, edited by Simon Doniger,
has done an effective job in bringing the two fields together.

Pope Pius XII, who once cautioned against psychoanalysis, recently came out in approval of it, calling it one of the weapons in the armory of modern healers.

A religious person may become emotionally ill, explains Dr. Leo Bartemeier, leading Catholic psychoanalyst, and former president of the American Psychiatric Association and the International Psychoanalytic Association.

"One may be a very holy person within himself and yet be torn with conflict," he says.

Dr. Karl Menninger, who with his brother, Dr. William Menninger, has been a leader in interpreting psychiatry and psychoanalysis to the troubled, tells of a remark made by a devout Catholic colleague as they were listening to a patient singing a hymn during a recital at a mental hospital.

"In how *many* different ways people pray," the Catholic psychiatrist said quietly.

The slow but sure union of psychoanalysis and religion brings to the troubled an even greater measure of happiness. They gain faith in the spiritual part of them that may have been stifled because they were fighting so desperately for their very psychological existence.

It takes time to give up the selfish needs that are part of this unreal fight. The troubled require an inordinate demand for attention because of the lack of proper attention as a child. The "specialness" each troubled person feels is caused by the lack of being "special" as a child, but this "specialness" must be relinquished if he wants to be happy as an adult.

"If everyone wanted applause, there would be no one left to applaud," an analyst reminded one man with a deep need for attention.

Sometimes you are apt to forget why you went into analysis as the days drag along and up go the eternal detours of defense.

"Always try to remember why you are here," an analyst advised one man.

"Why?" reflected the man. "I came to get relief from my asthma." Then he added, "But I see now that it's much more than that. I won't relieve my pain until I can grow up emotionally."

People grow up physically and intellectually but not emotionally if they have lived in fear. One of the most difficult struggles is to give up the anger and hatred which has served to fight fear.

One man, who nearly died after a heart attack, was asked by the analyst, "How do you feel?"

He looked at the analyst scornfully and said, "When I die, it will not be from a heart attack."

"What will you die from?" asked the analyst.

"I will die from misanthropy," he said bitterly.

He knew the depth of his anger at the human race, and more important, at himself. People die daily from accumulated anger only it is called other, more acceptable names, like heart trouble or high blood pressure. We call it anger only when it is murder or suicide, but the other is anger, too, a more unrecognizable, subtle anger, stemming from feeling unloved.

One man asked an analyst in wonder, "Why don't you ever get angry at some of the things I say to you?"

[131]

"Then I'd be no better off than you are," replied the analyst.

How long one undergoes analysis depends on his needs. Each one who seeks help is different. Some must have a long time to search the self.

"Why must troubled people go through such hell?" groaned one man.

"For heaven's sake, do you think everyone suffers as much as you do?" asked his analyst.

"I guess I do," he admitted. It had not occurred to him that some might not find the look at the inner self quite so difficult.

One man asked another, "How long did your analysis take you?"

"I stopped after five years—right in the middle of it," said the second. He was not joking, either. He found it so difficult to break through defenses that, even after five years, on reaching an impasse, he gave up.

"In six months I only started to scratch the surface of my psyche," said the first. "But as I got deeper and deeper, I went faster and faster. A year and a half was all I needed to feel good enough to go on by myself."

Some of the troubled may go to an analyst for two or three years, five times a week, or others as long as four or five years, three times a week. There is no time limit, although the average is probably two years, five times a week, or its equivalent.

In their suffering, some threaten to take their lives. The

good analyst knows when this threat is merely a dramatic device to get attention and when it is real.

"It occurred to me that if I went out the window one morning that would be some joke on you," one man taunted his analyst.

"I wouldn't think it was such a joke," replied the analyst. "I like you. I'd feel very sorry."

Then he added thoughtfully, "But just as the best of surgeons occasionally lose patients, so do we."

Another man insisted he was going to throw himself in New York's East River. "Then people will say what a terrible analyst you are," he told his analyst.

"Will *you* be any happier?" asked the analyst.

Both patients were saying, in effect, that if they killed themselves, it would reflect the analyst's failure. Failure to them was the worst possible disgrace. They had become safe enough to dare describe what they would like to do to their parents—give them a feeling of failure in return for the rigid demands imposed on them as children.

But the analysts were wise men who knew the terror that leads to thoughts of suicide. They knew these patients would not kill themselves even though they threatened to do so. They knew the feelings of suicide would disappear.

Analysis helps you to face how much you feel unloved. If you feel unloved, you believe you should be different from what you are and so you hate the way you are. You believe others must hate you and so you hate them. Hating others may also be a way to avoid hating yourself, a means of survival. For self-hate at its pitiless depths, may lead to self-destruction.

It is the ability to look at what you feel destructive and hateful about yourself that takes trust. You must trust the analyst more than anyone else you have known, because he is the one to whom you dare, for the first time in your life, describe such feelings as murder and suicide.

Analysis is not an "escape" from living. Those who need an escape find one without the help of an analyst. A troubled person usually has settled deep into escape from reality before he starts analysis. Analysis offers him the chance to know from what he escapes and give up the need to escape.

Analysis enhances creative ability. An artist freed of fear and anger is able to express not troubled but free feelings. The more conscious he is of the reasons why he paints or writes or composes, the more chance he has of enjoying what he creates. Desperate people show desperation, not freedom, in their work.

Analysis gives those who need it the strength to fight their own battles. Some lack that strength; others deceive themselves they have strength, not knowing it is false.

When someone says analysis "robs" you of strength, it is as though he is admitting *he* is easily robbed, as if he knows he must give up the mask of strength and uncover the weakness underneath should he face himself.

Analysis does not take anything from you. Instead, it gives an awareness of undeveloped strength within. It gives a sense of caring enough about the self so you may grow stronger.

It offers you a good dependence, that you may reach independence. There is no other route for the troubled.

How is it possible, Freud asked, to convince oneself of the "truth" of psychoanalysis? What is the proof that psychoanalysis does change people for the better?

There are no statistics to "prove" analysis works. This seems to bother some. We are a fact-finding nation, holding on grimly to facts as though they proved we were born—as though our heartbeat were not proof enough.

No one can "prove" how many have been helped how much by analysis. The proof of each analysis resides in the soul of a single man. Only he can tell if his pain is eased and how much. Others may know, to a lesser degree, for the effects of analysis are felt by those close to the one analyzed. We absorb ease and contentment just as we absorb anger and fury. When calmness has been absent and appears, we notice its presence. It ripples through a home, a community, a nation, a world, if strong enough.

Do the troubled get "cured" in analysis? If "cured" means "become a perfect human being," the answer is no. But the perfect human being is an illusion. Analysis helps the troubled feel less troubled.

There is no absolute in measuring the results of help. We must know how troubled a person was before he sought help, how much easier life becomes for him afterwards. We must consider each analysis by what the one who sought help felt he got out of it.

A number of men and women have become more warm, loving and civilized after analysis. They make such comments as: "I feel like a new person." "I want to live now—not die." "I know what it means to give love to someone." They describe how physical illnesses disappeared, how they live both in greater bodily and psychological ease.

It is not enough that physical symptoms disappear for one to feel materially better. Some help merely halts symptoms without changing the cause of the trouble. When symptoms disappear that may be only the start of help. Ulcers may go, but the body may rebel in another way if you do not lose the basic fear.

Some skeptics charge that analysis is "fashionable," as though fashion were a crime. Analysis *is* "fashionable"—luckily. What is wrong with fashion if it is a good one? All fashion fulfills a need and certain fashions exist forever if the need continues. The ideas of analysis have spread to movies, plays, books, television and radio and thus many have come to know there is a way out of deep suffering.

Perhaps it was "fashionable" at one time for a man to be inoculated against smallpox, but it saved his life. Psycho-analysis, which may be thought of as injections of love and trust, may also save lives.

Who should be analyzed? The answer depends on which analyst you ask. Some will help only the neurotic. Others will analyze the severely troubled, or psychotic.

The authorities have been wont to divide the troubled into two main categories—neurotic and psychotic. The neurotic, although harassed by troubled feelings, is still able to carry on his business and social life. The psychotic is so emotion-ally ill he often must be hospitalized.

The psychotic, who has lost control of his reason, may spend the rest of his days in a mental hospital, convinced that evil forces seek to kill him. The neurotic, who is in control of his reason, will not feel a victim of evil but he may be plagued by an occasional feeling that something wants to destroy him, he knows not what.

Freud described the difference thus: "In neurosis a part of reality is avoided by a sort of flight but in psychosis it [reality] is remodeled."

The psychotic cannot test reality because he feels so terrorized. It is true that some neurotics test it only with their toes, never daring to swim in it, but at least they recognize it and try to get acquainted with it.

Then there is what analysts call "the borderline" state, those who dwell in the netherland between neurosis and psychosis. While some will not treat the borderline, believing it better to let sleeping fantasies lie lest a man awake to his wrath and, in a fury, try to destroy himself or someone else, other analysts are not afraid to help a man no matter how troubled he may be.

No generalization can be made as to who can be helped. One analyst will spend years with a very troubled person, content with slow progress. He gets satisfaction in helping to bring someone back safely from the farthest psychic precipice. Another may prefer to spend less time with one man but help a larger number of the troubled.

Not everybody can change. While some find analysis nourishing and relatively painless, others discover it stirs up such psychic suffering that they are unable to endure it and must stop.

Just as there are successes, so there are failures, both because of the analyst and the troubled person. But this is no reason for us to give up faith in analysis. The demand for perfection stems from a sense of inner imperfection on the part of the unhappy, as though a perfect outside world would make up for crippled feelings.

But no profession is perfect, not the clergy, not the law, nor the medical profession. As an art-science, psychoanalysis is barely born. It was unknown in this country until 1908 when the late Dr. A. A. Brill and a few others started to practice.

Not every analyst can be 100 per cent successful with every troubled person. This is not Utopia. This is the highly emotionally-charged U.S.A.

Analysts are entitled to error, for they are human, not divine. There may be an unconscious need to play God in some of them, as in all healing professions, but civilization would be in far worse condition if there were no such need in men.

To the criticism that analysis deals with that most precious of all treasures, the human mind, and that anyone who touches it must be a master, there is but the reply that the human mind has taken a severe beating in the past few thousand years, and the fact that analysis, in some instances, is unable to relieve pain does not negate its value for the troubled.

We must ask, in addition to what makes a good analyst,

"What makes a good patient?" For two take part in this journey to happiness. The one who seeks help also shares the work.

"Analytic treatment makes as great demands for efforts on the part of the patient as on the physician, efforts to abolish the inner resistances," said Freud.

When analysts undertake to help someone, he said, they explain to him "the difficulties of the method, its long duration, the trials and sacrifices which will be required of him; and, as to the result, we tell him that we can make no definite promises, that success depends upon his endeavors, upon his understanding, his adaptability and his perseverance."

It is difficult to help some. Their anger and fear are so great they will take nobody's hand.

It is possible to have an unfortunate experience with an analyst. But this can be avoided, if proper care is taken in selecting the analyst. The choice must take into account the temperament of the prospective analyst along with the needs and problems of the one seeking help. The first interview is important. For here trust begins to be felt or its absence noted.

The beautiful, the successful and the wealthy may prove difficult to analyze because they have defenses of which society heartily approves. They may believe, "I have money, or beauty, or success and that's more than many others possess." They can coast along on the surface glitter.

Our country's analysts represent several different schools of thought. They divide chiefly into the Freudian and so-called non-Freudian. The Freudian group focus on the conflicts of childhood, primarily those which involve the feelings about survival and sexual fulfillment from infancy on.

The non-Freudians branch off in various directions. The William Alanson White group, for instance, accents "inter-personal relations," the impact of one person on another, consciously and unconsciously, and the need for each man to find "security." The Horney school emphasizes environment and culture as influencing man's behavior.

There are also the eclectics, who belong to no one school but integrate other philosophies with their own.

The reputable analysts use the basic theories of Freud even though they may add to them. It is only those who ignore Freud that are dangerous, those who toss away the whole and substitute, at best, a minute part. The part may look enticing, like frosting on a cake, but frosting without cake is scarcely a sensible food and may make a man ill if that is all he has as nourishment.

As Dr. Clara Thompson, of the William Alanson White group says, many of the troubled "achieve deep and lasting insight under or in spite of the various doctrines taught them, if in the interpersonal experience with the analyst the patient's genuine problems in living have been explored."

Some analysts work hard for harmony in the profession. The Psychiatric Forum Group in New York, for instance, brings together the various schools of thought in the city so members can exchange information and ideas on helping the troubled.

The important thing is that the analyst, no matter to which school he belongs, gives enough of a feeling of safety so you are able to reveal to yourself parts of yourself which have troubled you without your knowing why.

Before analysis you are apt to despise yourself for reasons you do not know. During analysis you start to know for what you despise yourself. After analysis you know you do not need to despise yourself, that you only did what you had to do and now, at long last, you may start out on your own, free from the distorted, loveless past.

Love of self and others is the great gift of psychoanalysis. It is the bridge to future happiness.

It brings, as a woman at the Menninger Clinic wrote:

Achievement

Acceptance of what has to be,
A muted joy in what I see
And hear and know and think and feel—
And living that again seems real.
When all these various things I find
Perhaps I'll call it peace of mind.

CHAPTER 10

What Means "Psychosomatic"?

MEN fight fear with anger, expressing anger in different ways. Some hurl anger outward, landing in prisons. Some turn anger inward on their minds, ending up in mental hospitals. Others thrust anger on their bodies and fall physically ill.

Anger will out. Nature protects us from excesses and when we are very angry we explode, either psychologically or physically.

For some, physical illness may be a way of hiding anger from themselves, of experiencing it in a more bearable way. Physical pain is preferable to facing severe psychic pain.

Today, many physical illnesses—such as ulcers, high blood pressure, tuberculosis, heart disease, allergies, arthritis, sinus —are being accepted as caused, in large part, by emotional problems. Some believe that all physical illness is related to the emotions, perhaps more deeply than we know.

We cannot separate the body, mind and emotions (emotions may be thought of, in a sense, as the spiritual connecting rods between body and mind). We react as a whole. When the mind reacts, so do the body and emotions. When the body reacts, so do the mind and emotions.

A troubled person fights with his whole being if he feels his life is threatened. If he has a physical problem, his mind and emotions try to solve it. If he has an emotional problem, his body and mind help out.

Physical illness may often be the body's attempt to solve an emotional problem which we are not consciously facing.

This was brought out dramatically in a study of 100 patients made by two Mayo Clinic psychiatrists. They warned physicians using ACTH and cortisone for the treatment of arthritis, rheumatic fever and other illnesses, to prescribe carefully and guard against personality changes in the patients. For they found that, although the physical illness was helped, one-third of the group became so emotionally troubled, they lost their minds temporarily.

The chronic, crippling physical illness had served as a defense against hidden, troubled feelings, explained Dr. Howard P. Rome who conducted the study with Dr. Francis J. Braceland. When the physical illness, or the defense, was suddenly removed, the troubled person found it so difficult to cope with reality that he had to resort to fantasy. The physical illness served as one way of keeping him alive; without it, he had to turn to another way—mental illness.

Physical illness, thus, may be a method of meeting unknown threats. The danger is that while it may temporarily ease deep, psychological pain, like alcohol or dope, in the long run it destroys. Truth becomes hidden even more solidly behind walls of physical as well as psychological pain.

Several groups are studying the relationship between emotional and physical disturbances. The Psychosomatic and Psychiatric Institute in Chicago, headed by Dr. Roy Grinker, is one of the pioneers.

Psychoanalysis is changing the whole of medicine. Many physicians are starting to understand that emotional difficulties may lead to physical illness and to recommend psychological help when needed.

Doctors traditionally have focussed on the physical side of illness. Physical illness is their intellectual and vested interest. But they should not be blind to the harm that may occur if they by-pass the emotions.

We may well ask how many of the 19,000,000 who entered the nation's hospitals last year received the help they really needed, and how many others who saw doctors in offices and in homes were properly diagnosed?

The physicians' own publication, the Journal of the American Medical Association, offers instances of needless surgery and of persons treated for organic illness who should have been given help for emotional problems.

Emotional disturbances were present in 47 per cent of 2,038 hospital patients, according to a study made by Dr. Bernard I. Lewis of the Department of Internal Medicine, State University of Iowa College of Medicine, reporting in the Oct. 25, 1952, issue of the Journal.

Twenty-five per cent of all who go to general hospitals suffer from emotional disturbances which are treated "under various other diagnoses," according to another article appearing in the Journal on Jan. 17, 1953.

"Often we have heard a physician condemn the patient for being a troublesome neurotic, and in the same breath order more exhaustive X-ray studies," say the authors, Dr. A. E. Bennett, Dr. Eugene A. Hargrove and Bernice Engle, of Berkeley, California.

They maintain that some doctors are unwilling to admit there is more than a bodily illness, that there is a "person in the body" who may need help with emotional problems. This refusal to diagnose psychiatrically, or the inability to do it, is responsible for some of the present high cost of medical treatment, they said.

Two years before, in an article carried in the Journal on Nov. 10, 1951, the same authors reported on a study of 500 people covered by voluntary prepayment admitted to a general hospital. They wanted to find out how many with emotional disturbances were mistakenly treated for bodily disorders and the amount spent for the patients by the prepayment plans.

They discovered 10 per cent showed "definite emotional illnesses treated as organic disturbances" and another 5 per cent had "minimum organic findings and needed psychiatric evaluation" before a decision to operate was made.

They also studied another 500 patients, 150 of whom had emotional disturbances but were admitted "under various diagnoses of serious organic diseases." The group included 244 who underwent surgical operations.

One woman diagnosed as "menopausal syndrome" disguised "a full-blown involutional melancholia" and was treated, without relief, by dilatation and curettage, for which the prepayment plan paid $130. The diagnosis of chronic appendicitis "often" covered frank "conversion hysterias," they declared, and not infrequently hemorrhoidectomy was done when, in the opinion of the authors, the patient's anxiety or depression was probably the cause of the physical symptom and psychiatry was indicated rather than surgery. Colitis was often treated purely as a physical symptom with "complete neglect of psychic tension states," they asserted.

They went on to say that instances where surgery or medicine was used in this way to try to cure what were really emotional disorders were "frequent." Errors of diagnosis in this group of 500 cost the prepayment plans many thousands of dollars, they reported. It also was costly in needless suffering to the patient who was not helped with his basic problem.

It is ironic that proof of what some have known intuitively for years is now substantiated because prepayment plans thought there might be abuse of the protection they provide. Sometimes it takes a wallop in our wallet to awaken our heart to truth. On the basis of the above study, the cost of prepayment to the public might be less if diagnostic and mental health services were included as a basic benefit.

Psychiatrists do save some from surgery. One man, lying in Mt. Sinai Hospital, New York, awaiting an operation on his sinus, started talking to the psychiatrist who accompanied the physician on his rounds in the wards.

"I've been intending to get help," he said wistfully. "Just never got around to it."

"Why don't you begin now?" suggested the psychiatrist. "If your sinus isn't too bad, you might postpone the operation."

The man agreed. The psychiatrist arranged for him to get help at one of the hospital's psychiatric clinics. After several months the man found his sinus condition so improved no operation was necessary.

Needless surgery and wrong diagnosis occur not only because doctors ignore the emotions but because the troubled choose to go to doctors rather than psychiatrists. They fear the latter more than they do physicians.

Some know they are more afraid of psychic than of physical pain. A well-known politician, suffering severe ulcers, admitted he needed emotional help.

"It would probably clear up my ulcers," he said. "But I'm more scared of what I would find in my soul than I am of my blasted stomach bleeding."

Others deny that physical and emotional pain have a strong bond.

"It hurts me here," they say, touching a muscle or patch

of skin. "This is real hurt." As though psychological hurt is not real.

Why do they hurt in that particular spot? At that particular time? Why do others not hurt? What does the physical hurt mean to them in terms of their whole life? Is it a way of punishing themselves? Of punishing others? Is it a way of feeling sorry for themselves? Of getting sympathy? A way out of responsibility? A way of escaping other feelings?

It is interesting to note that the same pattern of illness often runs in a family. Doctors say this occurs because a physical constitution is inherited. But analysts find that some unconsciously choose the illness of the parent they most admire, imitation, even unto illness, being the sincerest form of flattery.

Physical illnesses often clear up entirely or are relieved when a person gets help for troubled feelings. This has been shown time and again.

A man whose arthritis disappeared after analysis remarked, "It doesn't seem right to live without physical pain. I have to get used to a new feeling." He had faced a different kind of pain. With the ability to stand psychological pain, he lost the physical pain that served as a warning of the other, more significant pain.

"*It doesn't seem right to live without pain,*" he said. That is one of the tragedies of the troubled. Feeling good does not seem right because it is unfamiliar. Pain is the familiar.

Little children are still leading the way. "My heart hurts," a small boy told an analyst.

"Have you been to see a doctor?" the analyst asked.

"Not *that* kind of hurt," said the boy scornfully. "Doctors can't help my hurt."

But doctors can help, if they will know that all kinds of hurt may go together.

But better that doctors stay away completely from the realm of help for the troubled than to dole out such advice as the following, which appeared in an issue of the Journal of the American Medical Association in the column, "Queries and Minor Notes":

Too Little Romance

To the Editor:—A man, aged 31, has been married 11 years. The couple had three children in the early years of marriage. He now complains of almost complete lack of sexual response from his wife, who is in excellent health. She rarely reaches a climax. One physician suggested that her condition might be due to subconscious fear of pregnancy, which resulted in a sterilizing procedure, followed by no improvement. This condition has existed since the beginning of the marriage. Is there any preparation that might cause improvement?

Answer.—The fact that this wife does sometimes reach a climax shows that she can respond, which points to faulty sexual technique on the part of the husband. The removal of fear of pregnancy by sterilization is further indication that the husband must be an amateur. He should become informed on sex techniques and correct his inexperience. If the wife sometimes reacts and sometimes does not, it appears that the husband's timing is poor and that he is sometimes premature. He should make it his business to see that his wife is sufficiently prepared before attempting consummation of the act. The attempt to correct this problem seems to have been misdirected, as is often the case. There probably is too little romance in this union.

If only the explanation were this easy—"too little romance!" The physician who sterilized the wife showed little awareness of the real need—love and understanding that would help both husband and wife to overcome the fear of their own bodies and the sex act.

No real help was given two troubled people who sought relief of psychological pain. Rather, their unhappiness brought them further unhappiness. They were punished for being unhappy.

There are heartening signs that the medical and psychiatric professions are working more closely. A number of medical schools are including intensive psychiatric and psychoanalytic courses in the training of young doctors so they may understand how "the whole person," not just the body, is involved in illness.

A comprehensive study of this question, including recommendations by leaders in both medical and psychiatric fields, is contained in a book, *Psychiatry and Medical Education,* published by the American Psychiatric Association.

Medical students should be helped to solve their own emotional problems, for if a doctor is "frustrated and maladjusted, he cannot do his job well," the book suggests at one point.

It finds that "there is disturbing evidence" that many medical students "tend to undergo a hardening process and become insensitive to the emotional needs of their fellow human beings" while in medical school. Medical students, particularly in their first year, are subject to a large amount of anxiety. A study of one class showed that almost 50 per cent of the students had emotional "handicaps constituting a serious problem in mental health."

The book implies that as doctors become more aware of their own emotional problems, they will be more aware of emotional problems in others. "Et tu, Brute!" applies to the physician.

The School of Medicine at Emory University, Atlanta, Georgia, schedules each medical student in his freshman and sophomore years to take part in group therapy classes. A number have gone on to individual therapy. The program is designed, as Dr. Carl A. Whitaker, chairman of the department of psychiatry at the School of Medicine, explains, to help the doctor develop an increasing capacity "to be psychotherapeutic in all he does with his patients."

It is not always the doctors who have been against psychoanalysis. An amusing statement appeared in a paper on "Japanese Psychiatry and Psychotherapy" presented at the annual American Psychiatric Association convention in 1952. The authors, Dr. Avrohm Jacobson, Chief of the Neuropsychiatric Service, 141st General Hospital, Kyushu, Japan, and Albert N. Berenberg, clinical psychologist at the Osaka Army Hospital, Osaka, Japan, reported: "Most of the members of the analytic association in Japan are not only untrained in analysis, but quite anti-analytic."

In this country, probably most of the members of the analytic associations are pro-analytic, but it would not be true to say that all psychiatrists are pro-analytic. Certainly those who give wholesale electro-shock or those who talk "at" people rather than help them discover what lies in themselves cannot be called pro-analytic.

The medical profession has come quite a way in accepting psychoanalysis if one considers how doctors rose in wrath the first evening Freud described his findings before the Academy of Medicine in Vienna.

Freud lived for years as an outcast of the medical profession which refused to accept his theories. At one point he told a group of young doctors:

". . . a psychological attitude of mind is still foreign to you, and you are accustomed to regard it with suspicion, to deny it a scientific status, and to leave it to the general public, poets, mystics, and philosophers. Now this limitation in you is undoubtedly detrimental to your medical efficiency; for on meeting a patient it is the mental aspects with which one first comes into contact, as in most human relationships, and I am afraid you will pay the penalty of having to yield a part of the curative influence at which you aim to the quacks, mystics, and faith-healers whom you despise."

He proved a prophet on this, as on other things he predicted. One reason the troubled seek out "quacks," "mystics" and "faith-healers" is because the men of medical science do not help as effectively as they might.

CHAPTER 11

The Fist of Falsity

NOTHING is so intangible as trouble, nothing so tenacious once it takes hold. Only those who know what they do should give help. Otherwise they may harm.

In their suffering, men are apt to grab for any help offered. It is no wonder short-cut, dramatic, sometimes phoney methods find followers. The troubled may be so desperate they will try anything. Also, they may be in such misery they are not able to know whether help is the right kind.

[155]

The danger, and there usually is danger in the quick, thoughtless way, is that unsound help may step up suffering. It may also delay or destroy faith in real help.

"The mission of those who would replace passion by reason and prejudice by understanding in human affairs is one of the most important in the world. The field in which we have to work is rich with promise."

The author of England's health and social insurance plan, Lord Beveridge, might have added after the phrase "rich with promise," the words "although young in origin."

For the knowledge how to change a man's feeling and thinking so he may become more reasonable is of recent birth. Its growth, like all natural growth, holds awkward stages and is open to abuse.

Three main hazards confront the troubled person. First, there is the charlatan who deliberately masquerades as an authority when neither his background nor qualifications entitle him to give help. He attracts our attention occasionally when headlines scream of the exposure of someone pretending to be a psychoanalyst, psychiatrist or psychologist, who has been hauled into court by some troubled person and charged with unethical practices.

Then there is the expert who does not misrepresent himself but who cannot help anyone feel better. He possesses all the proper qualifications but has not faced his own struggles deeply enough. He is too troubled to help the troubled.

Lastly, there is the small "lunatic fringe" of the psychiatric and psychological professions which attracts, one might suspect, the "lunatic fringe" of the public. Every profession has this sore spot and it would be unrealistic to expect psychiatry and psychology to be immune.

The American public is fleeced out of roughly (or roughly fleeced out of) more than $375,000,000 a year by "psychological quacks" who give unsound advice. This is the estimate of Fillmore Sanford, executive secretary of the American Psychological Association.

There are at least 25,000 persons who advertise they give help on emotional problems, many of whom are untrained, incompetent or "outright quacks." In 1951 the New York City classified telephone directory listed seventy-three individuals and thirty-seven organizations under the heading "psychologists." Only a third of the individuals belonged to the American Psychological Association and many of the organizations failed to meet the standards established by the Association.

"Psychiatric quacks" are "swindling" the public out of millions each year, Dr. Morris Fishbein, former editor of the Journal of the American Medical Association, charged at a meeting of the American Psychiatric Association. Studies he conducted in Chicago and Los Angeles indicated "a terrific number of bogus practitioners" advising and acting as consultants on emotional problems.

He called on the psychiatrists of the nation to combat these "quacks." He said the field of medicine had eliminated the majority of its "quacks" through restrictive legislation, but psychiatry lacked such legislation.

"What abuse is leveled at psychiatry affects the entire profession," he chided the psychiatrists. He insisted it was necessary that every part of the medical profession "sustain a high standard of training and morale."

The money spent uselessly by unhappy persons runs into hundreds of millions each year. The wasted money is tragic enough but more tragic is the compounding of suffering that accompanies it, for which no amount of dollars can compensate.

In their desperation and confusion the troubled will ask help from a taxi driver, plumber, engineer, and of anyone who sets himself up as an expert on love, marriage, sex.

These who seek such two-bit therapists only ask for further unhappiness. The self-styled "authorities" may use the language of psychiatry and psychology but they do not know its meaning. They often give advice that adds anxiety.

For instance, they urge some who are single to get married when marriage may only increase their misery unless they first face their troubled feelings. Those who expect marriage to solve their problems only build further unhappiness. Marriage forces one to face the self in merciless fashion.

These "experts" do not know a cardinal principle of help —you do not hit someone in his defenses. When the troubled come out of fear seeking love, you do not punish them for being afraid.

A well-known radio personality who has been giving "advice" for years over air that, by now, must be slightly polluted, causes needless suffering by inducing the troubled to expose themselves to his cock-eyed counsel. They come to him hoping for sympathy. Sometimes they leave in tears, feeling they have made a public spectacle of themselves to no avail.

Some are too prone to take the word of the one who sets himself up as an authority, that he is an authority. This dependency is part of feeling troubled.

"Surely advice on emotional problems is more important than pills for a stomach ache, and yet anyone without status can put out a sign saying he is a psychologist, no matter what kind of a crackpot he may be, and anyone may come and ask his advice on important emotional matters," pointed out the late Dr. E. H. L. Corwin, executive secretary of the Public Health Relations Committee of the New York Academy of Medicine.

One way of protecting the troubled is to license those who give help, as physicians are licensed. Today anyone may hang up a shingle announcing he is an analyst, psychologist, counselor or guidance expert, and no one can say him nay except in the state of Kentucky and the city of San Diego, Cal. They have licensing laws for psychologists.

Connecticut and Virginia are the two states providing for certification of psychologists, but this applies only to clinical psychologists, those most closely allied to the medical profession. Certification allows only the qualified to use the title "psychologist." Licensing, a stronger measure, imposes penalties on those who practice without a license which is granted after an examination. Certification laws do not stop the psychological fraud from practicing, but they do provide the troubled with a guide.

Licensing of psychologists is no simple matter. It opens

up the question of questions—whether those who do not possess a medical degree should give help with emotional problems.

Until a few years ago most psychological help was given by psychiatrists to the severely troubled in mental hospitals. But psychoanalysis has widened the frontiers, bringing help to the less troubled to prevent serious illness from developing.

Also, with greater acceptance of the bond between mind and body, a number of the physically ill are now seeking emotional help when physicians fail to relieve their symptoms more than temporarily.

Because of this greater demand, "counselling and guidance" has come into being, given chiefly by psychologists and social workers, as distinguished from "therapy," given by psychiatrists and psychoanalysts.

"Counseling and guidance" are for the person who may be slightly troubled for the moment but who is not deeply disturbed, according to the medical profession. "Therapy" is for the severely emotionally ill and only those with a medical degree are qualified to give it, the medical profession insists.

Who is to decide where the psychic line is drawn? When does "counseling and guidance" spill over into therapy? Some say that anyone who asks another to help him out with a problem, no matter how minor, is asking for therapy. Others disagree, declaring the degree of troubled feelings indicates different degrees of help.

The American Psychiatric Association recently issued a strong statement warning against the licensing of any profession other than the medical to treat "mental ailments." It held that "therapy" was a province of the medical profession.

"The association recognizes that the skills of other professional groups, psychologists, ministers, teachers, lawyers and social workers, are essential and useful in terms of their objectives and methods," declared Dr. D. Ewen Cameron, president of the association. "However, these groups do not assume responsibility for the health of the patient as does the physician. A physician may utilize the services of other disciplines but he cannot delegate his medical responsibility."

A psychiatrist or psychoanalyst may assign responsibility to a "non-medical person" who carries out treatment under his supervision, the medical profession says. But the "non-medical man" may not give therapy on his own.

Yet a number who do not possess medical degrees openly practice therapy without being supervised by a psychiatrist or psychoanalyst. Among them are lay analysts, psychologists and social workers.

Psychologists and social workers, for the most part, give only supportive help. But lay analysts practice psychoanalysis.

Freud believed that a lay analyst, if he had enough experience with the troubled and if his own analysis was successful, could be as competent as the man who went through medical school.

According to Theodor Reik, one of the foremost proponents of lay analysis in this country, Freud once remarked, "I am a decided enemy of lay analysis—by physicians."

Dr. Reik maintains it is "inevitable" that lay analysts eventually will be allowed to practice here without opposition. In

Europe they are accepted freely but in this country the psychiatric and psychoanalytic groups, generally, oppose them.

The American Psychoanalytic Association, in spite of the expressed attitude of Freud approving of lay analysts and the fact that European psychoanalytic societies take in lay analysts, now accepts for membership only those with a medical degree. (Except those in under the "grandfather" clause—members before the restriction went into effect.)

One argument against allowing those without medical degrees to give help is that since there are no licensing laws, the medical degree at least provides the public with a minimum safeguard. Someone without a medical degree may give excellent help but there is just as much chance he will not be able to help at all and might even hurt.

There is the argument, too, that because lay analysts lack a medical degree they may not be aware of the severity or even the presence of physical illness.

A suggestion has been made that those who go to lay analysts first receive a physical examination from a physician. (It seems unlikely that in this land of hypochondria most of the troubled would not have had at least one visit to a physician before winding up at an analyst's office.)

Another suggestion is that lay analysts be used only when the troubled are referred to them by psychiatrists and psychoanalysts.

The main argument for lay analysis is that the one who helps the troubled needs a deep understanding of the emotions more than he needs a medical degree, since he is dealing primarily with the psyche. Some believe that as the demand for help becomes even greater and the influence of the American Medical Association perhaps less, medical training may be by-passed for a thorough grounding in the social sciences plus a personal analysis.

Dr. Lawrence Kubie, a member of the New York Psychoanalytic Institute which has been described as the guardian of Freudian analysis in this country, has made an interesting proposal. He has suggested there be a "pilot test" of a new curriculum, to be conducted under the joint auspices of a medical school and a university department of psychology. It would contain essential courses from the medical curriculum, courses in the psychological and social sciences, and psychoanalytic training, and would take seven to nine years after graduation from college. On completion of such a course the individual would be licensed to do psychodiagnosis and psychotherapy *only* in association with a physician.

Such an idea will probably take a while to put into being, if it ever is, for strong opposition still rages.

Perhaps the important issue in the whole matter of help is the crucial one raised by Dr. William Menninger as he spoke to the psychologists of the nation at their annual meeting.

He said: "Theoretically, psychotherapy is indicated for the maladjusted or ill person; counseling is indicated for the healthy person who seeks advice about a specific problem, assumed to be minor in nature."

"Assumed" is the key word. For, Dr. Menninger went on to say:

"Such a differentiation becomes tenuous to many of us

who think of marital problems, problems of child relation-ships, speech handicaps, reading disabilities, educational mal-adjustments and many other human problems as having a very definite relationship to mental health."

Urging every clinical psychologist, "whether or not he practices psychotherapy," to become acquainted with thera-peutic principles, Dr. Menninger warned: *"His examination in most, if not in all cases, is a kind of therapy and any con-tact with the patient has therapeutic implications."* (Italics are the author's.)

The one who gives advice can do so effectively only inso-far as he has some recognition of the operation of the uncon-scious, of the subtle relationships that exist between people and of "symbolic meanings in a psychological examination," Dr. Menninger held.

He was making the point that help, no matter how minor, which fails to take into account unconscious behavior, is not help.

The one who helps must be aware of the power of the un-conscious. Otherwise the troubled might just as well take to tea leaves and fortune-tellers.

Some who give help are stumbling around in the psycho-logical dark ages. They act as though the spoken word al-ways stood for true feelings and thoughts. Sometimes we say what we would like to believe, or feel we should believe, rather than what we truly believe.

Some who profess to help have little or no understanding of how the unconscious may drive a man. They think they can change someone if only they talk "at" him loud and long

[164]

enough. One psychologist complained of a man who sought help, "I don't understand why he keeps doing things I tell him *not* to do."

If brief instruction were enough, we'd all be happy as happy kings. We have to care about ourselves first in order to change. And the caring does not come via a command.

Wrong help over a period of time will cause needless misery, although there is another side to the coin of pain. The troubled have strong defenses and it may take a while before further psychological damage is done. One may argue, too, that they would suffer anyhow. The point is, they are paying for relief of suffering and should be entitled to a fair chance at healing.

The troubled must watch for those who are so troubled themselves they cannot help others. Because a man has been troubled, does not mean he cannot give help. If he has faced his troubled feelings, he can help. The troubled, once they pull away from pain, are not apt to forget its agony. The true healer may have tasted of emotional death; that may be one reason he cares about preventing others from dying emotionally. Some who give help have faced their inner selves so completely they possess the understanding "which passeth all understanding."

What should you look for when you seek someone to help you?

There are two main considerations: personal qualities and professional qualifications. Both are important.

You might ask such questions as: Does he seem a kindly person? Do you get the feeling he is interested in you, rather than in promoting his own theories? Does he intellectualize or does he talk simply and directly? Do you feel you can trust him? Does he seem confident of himself in a quiet way? Does he give you a feeling of ease?

Or does he appear arrogant and blustery? Does he give orders? Does he make you feel more tense and nervous? Does he seem over-anxious, wanting to make an impression on you? Is he cynical and wisecracking?

Does money seem more important to him than you feel it should? It is realistic for everyone to want to earn a good living. But those who really help get satisfaction from the help they give even more than from material reward. If they do not, they cannot help the troubled.

There are some obvious danger signs that most people would heed. For instance, they would avoid going to anyone who advertised as follows:

"Hypnotism and Suggestion to Make You Happier"

"Metaphysician—Healing, Marriages Performed, Problems Adjusted"

"Astrological Interpretation of Human Needs"

"Personal Problems, Career, Mental Healing, Hindu, Yoga"

"Processing by Professional Auditors Leading to the Re-Evaluation of the Sub-conscious and Reactive Mind for Better Survival"

"Psychometaphysical Healing"

A type of man to guard against is the one who administers a fixed system of treatment for all the troubled. Dr. Robert Knight, psychoanalyst, in warning against this kind of help, says: "This is true whether it refers to those therapists who treat all patients with such banal exhortations as 'Buck up,' 'Go home and forget it,' 'Stop worrying about that,' 'Pull yourself together,' 'Don't cross bridges until you come to them,' and so on; to therapists who treat all patients by assigning reading for subsequent interview discussions in prepared booklets on how to live; to psychoanalysts who put all patients on the couch and tell them to free-associate; or to therapists who keep the syringe loaded with sodium pentothal for each patient, or who routinely start their hypnotic maneuvers promptly.

"One may give insulin to every diabetic, or operate every acute appendix, with, of course, some judgment as to dosage, timing, and collateral measures, but psychotherapy is, or should be, a highly individual matter for each patient. Far too often in current practice the type of psychotherapy used with the patient is determined solely by the limited training and ability of the psychotherapist rather than by either the type of illness the patient has or the type of patient that has the illness."

Each one who seeks help should investigate carefully the one who gives help as guarantee against his being either charlatan or incompetent.

The troubled person may be referred to someone by a friend or family doctor. He should make an additional check on professional qualifications, no matter how dependable the referral may seem.

One measure of professional standing is membership in the national association that represents the group and which sets standards for its members. There is the American Psychiatric Association for psychiatrists, the American Psychoanalytic Association comprised of psychoanalysts, the American Psychological Association for psychologists, and the American Association of Social Workers for social workers.

Detailed information on each psychiatrist and psychoanalyst, his training and experience, is available through county medical societies. It may be obtained from the society's registry or by calling at its office. The directories of the American Psychiatric Association, the American Psychoanalytic Association and the American Psychological Association will list the background and qualifications of each member. They will also disclose whether he is a "diplomate," that is, has passed examinations given by a board within the association, qualifying him as a specialist in his field.

The one seeking help can also ask other experts in the field whom he may know about the person he selects. He may also check with the local or state mental hygiene society, listed in the telephone directory, which will refer him to a competent man. If there is no local mental hygiene society, the state mental hygiene society will know of help available in the neighborhood. (A list of the state societies is given in the appendix.)

In a large city, one may call the Council of Social Agencies or Welfare Council or whatever group coordinates the city's welfare agencies. A family or welfare agency in the vicinity should also be able to give details about help.

For those who live in a small town or rural area, the County Department of Welfare or the County Public Health

Nursing Office will furnish information as to where good help is available.

Each state has a mental hygiene department, a division of government to which all of us contribute as taxpayers, which is charged with the responsibility for developing resources for helping the troubled. Generally located in the capital of the state, this department can be reached by letter or telephone.

The troubled should refuse to accept the incompetent, both in private consultation and in clinics.

"People have been compromising in order to get staffs for clinics," warns Dr. Abraham Barhash, former director of community clinics for the National Association for Mental Health. "Inadequately trained psychiatrists may harm those they see, and their presence in the clinic closes the door for a more competent psychiatrist."

All the available information may still not guarantee the best in help. Some psychoanalysts do not belong to the American Psychoanalytic Association, for instance, but are members of the American Orthopsychiatric Association, which is concerned primarily with child psychiatry. Some belong to no group at all, yet are capable.

The reverse may also be true—some may possess the highest academic and professional standing and not be particularly helpful.

Luck probably plays its part here, as in most things in life. But "luck belongs to the good card player" as Bernard Baruch once told Isabel Leighton, a writer who is active in the mental health field. Luck may belong to the one who searches for the man he feels is right for him and makes no compromise.

The troubled person at first may not like the one he has selected, but later start to like him. Or he may like him at first and then grow to dislike him. If the dislike is consistent, he had better go elsewhere. Sometimes those who give help succeed with one person but fail with another.

Each relationship stands or falls by itself. Generalizations about who can help whom, perhaps help no one. Just as each troubled person is different, so is each one who helps. To lump in categories for the sake of convenience is to be expedient at the sacrifice of individual dignity.

The professions themselves might give more guidance to the troubled. For instance, they might go on record against certain kinds of help or certain persons who, they believe, increase rather than ease emotional pain.

Some psychiatrists and psychoanalysts will discuss among themselves the perils of specific types of treatment but will take no official stand, either individually or through their organizations. This corridor criticism does not help the troubled tell the difference between harmful and effective help.

If, as psychiatrists say, public education is necessary to eliminate some of the misunderstanding and abuses, it would seem they have a responsibility to inform us about some of the hazards.

The American Psychological Association has shown courage in unmasking mental health monstrosities. When no other group would act, it called on psychologists, "in the public interest," not to use the techniques "peculiar" (word well chosen) to Dianetics, a so-called approach to mental health conceived by L. Ron Hubbard. The claims made by Mr. Hubbard, described by his publishers as "mathematician and theoretical philosopher," are incompatible with sense or science. He asserted in his preface that he discovered a technique that would "invariably cure all psychosomatic ills and human aberrations." The world still waits.

The association has just completed another undertaking in the public interest—a code of ethics designed to raise the standards of psychologists—because it has been concerned by the number who, with all the good will in the world, make unwise decisions as a result of lack of experience or knowledge.

The code represents a frank, honest appraisal of the profession, by the profession, for the profession. It presents examples where psychologists gave wrong advice. It outlines what the ethical decision would have been.

"In this code psychologists have used their own tool of research to draw up standards for themselves," explained Dr. Nicholas Hobbs, chairman of the Committee on Ethical Standards which conducted the four-year project financed by funds from the Rockefeller Foundation.

The psychologists felt they wanted a standard that "would make a difference in their day-by-day practice as well as take care of persons on the fringe," he said.

To try to guarantee the emotional fitness of psychologists the Department of Guidance and Personnel Administration of the School of Education at New York University has asked those who wish their Ph.D. in counselling to be interviewed by the University's psychiatrist after successful completion of various examinations. The staff of the department then meets with the psychiatrist to discuss each candidate. Dr. Robert Hoppock, professor of education at the University, reports that, "to our pleasant surprise, the independent judgments of the psychiatrist and of a clinical psychologist on our staff have been identical in almost every case."

The matter of responsibility to the public in a broad sense is often discussed by the groups which give help. Marian Mc-Bee, of the National Association of Mental Health, the first psychiatric social worker to become president of the American Orthopsychiatric Association several years ago, brought this up at the annual meeting.

Declaring that human behavior can be influenced for evil as well as good, she said it was not enough for those who give help to find out the facts, leaving their application to others. She asked the members to give leadership in trying to apply knowledge of human behavior "to the ever-increasing problems of people who want to live together comfortably and at peace."

One question sometimes raised is whether all the publicity given emotional help is desirable. Will publicity help people lead happier lives?

Most of the material put out to "educate" the public does little but add to the existing confusion, Dr. Jules Coleman, psychoanalyst, has said. "On the whole, the material is so alarmistic, places so much emphasis on the prevalence of emotional disturbances, the complexity of the dangers which are normally encountered and the likelihood and ease of invoking disaster for anybody's future mental health, that the net result must be to produce uncertainty, confusion and distress," he told a meeting of the American Orthopsychiatric Association. He warned that "knowledge does not cure" and made the important point that "there is no easy preventive formula to substitute for the hard road of skilled treatment."

Dr. Coleman is right; the troubled are not helped to feel better by printed words. On the other hand, perhaps the words may aid in laying the groundwork for help. The day-by-day job of interpreting and presenting to the troubled ways in which their emotional pain may be eased may make it easier to get more people to give help. As the demand increases, it is likely that the number who give help will increase.

Publicity can point up the need for more competent men and women to help the troubled. It can also aid in breaking down some of the fear of accepting help.

Newspapers have been educating the public by describing some of the methods of help and warning against the dangers. At one time psychiatrists fled reporters. Today most of the press and psychiatrists work in harmony, thanks to the efforts of the American Psychiatric Association. Its public information committee, Dr. Daniel Blain, medical director, and Robert Robinson, assistant for administration and public relations, have been largely responsible for the progress. The American Psychoanalytic Association and the American Psychological Association, also have opened doors wide to reporters.

All this is guiding the troubled. But each one seeking help

needs to use his own wisdom in selecting the one who is to help. The least he can do is to search for the best help available (which is not necessarily the most expensive), just as he would go to the best heart specialist if he suffered heart trouble. If he is intent enough on getting good help he is likely to find it, even though he may have to wait for it.

To put trust in another to advise us on the most delicate matters of living is tribute, indeed. But tribute is not enough. We must also use judgment in selecting the one who is to give help.

It is vital we know when the velvet of the helping glove is extended with the iron fist of falsity inside.

CHAPTER 12

Outposts of Terror

THE care of the severely troubled has always presented
society with a dilemma. In ancient days the emotionally
disturbed were thought possessed by the devil or some ma-
levolent spirit. They were cast aside and often brutally treated,
chained in cellars and beaten. Even today a number are punished when they become violent, put in strait jackets or isolation cells.

Because there has been no deep conviction as to why men

become troubled, their care has not developed as fully or as judiciously as it might. Our nation is proud of its fight for physical health but it has not really faced the problem of emotional health. We spend millions of dollars on heart disease, infantile paralysis, cancer, but a relatively very small amount on mental illness—our largest medical problem and allied to most other medical problems.

We have not given much thought to those who live in a state which Dr. Robert Felix, director of the National Mental Health Institute, described as "death without rigor mortis."

He had just walked through a mental hospital when this phrase came to mind. He watched face after face turned to him in despair or desperation, fury or emptiness. He saw shells of people mocking the motions of living. He thought of them the day they were born, experiencing what he called "one of the two miracles of life," and looked at them as they were now, "denied the second miracle, death." They dwelled in half-death, suspended between living and dying.

For those who are so emotionally ill they need to be hospitalized, there is available the private mental hospital, usually called a sanitarium, and the public state hospital. Those who can afford it usually choose the sanitarium where more often care is intensive and the latest in treatment is offered.

Psychoanalysis and psychoanalytic therapy (help based on the principles of psychoanalysis) are being successfully used at such private hospitals as Chestnut Lodge Sanitarium, Rockville, Maryland; High Point Hospital, Port Chester, New York; Hillside Hospital, Queens, New York, and the Menninger Clinic, Topeka, Kansas.

A few private hospitals also use psychoanalysts in private practice to help the severely troubled.

The private hospitals are expensive, ranging from $100 to $1000 a week (the average runs about $200 or $300), which means only those with money can afford them. They do accept a small percentage of patients at lower cost, however.

Most of the nation's severely troubled, 650,000 of them, live in the public mental hospitals which are supported by tax funds. And, as with most welfare which is tax-supported, they are under-financed. We might say that, with the money they receive, they are doing the best job possible as far as custodial care goes. But they give very little of the treatment that seems to help the most—verbal help—because of the shortage of psychiatrists.

"Judged not against the almshouses they were one hundred years ago, but on what they could be doing, our mental institutions have failed miserably in giving their patients what modern medicine has to offer," says Dr. George S. Stevenson, medical director of the National Association for Mental Health, who has worked long and hard to improve both conditions in mental hospitals and the country's community facilities for the care of the less troubled.

The feeling that leads people to remark with a shudder, "It makes me sick just to think of a mental hospital," holds back, in large part, the development of care for the severely troubled, he believes.

We isolate our mental hospitals, hiding them in remote hills and valleys, making it difficult for relatives to visit patients and for administrators to get staff. The isolation also

[177]

sets the hospitals apart psychologically from the rest of us. We still consider them outposts of terror rather than places where kindness and psychological skill may help the tormented.

We treat the severely troubled without dignity even before they reach the hospitals. They go through unpleasant and harmful experiences in many states while awaiting admission according to a report on the nation's mental hospitals published by the Council of State Governments and written by Brevard Crihfield. They are herded into jail while awaiting disposition in thirty-five states, and made to endure trial by jury in others, notes the report, called "The Mental Health Programs of the Forty-Eight States." Texas and Mississippi are the states with the most archaic laws, still requiring trial by jury. States with the most humane laws are those in which only a certificate by two physicians is needed for admission. The report suggests states adopt a model law prepared by the National Institute of Mental Health.

We treat our severely troubled as though they had committed crimes rather than as though they were emotionally ill. The very word "commit" connotes criminality. Hauled into courtrooms, they stand "accused" when they should be thought of as troubled and needing understanding help.

After they leave the hospitals, we make them feel even more defeated. It is as though we expected them to be helped by snarls.

Men and women, discharged from Brooklyn State Hospital, New York, anxiously asked Dr. Nathaniel Breckir, who conducted group therapy classes, such questions as:

"Shall I tell my boss I was a patient in a mental hospital?"
"I am going out with a girl. Is it necessary for me to let her
know I had shock treatment?" "My parents are bad for me.
They tell me not to come here any more. Shall I leave them?"
"When people speak of someone's being 'nutty' or 'crazy,'
what shall I say?"

We are fortunate in our pioneers who are willing to stand
up and be counted for courage in saying to the world: "Here
is a fear we all must face if we are to know the way to inner
and outer peace."

Clifford Beers charted the path of courage in *A Mind
That Found Itself*, when he described his harrowing experiences in a mental hospital and founded an organization to
improve conditions, now called The National Association for
Mental Health. He showed that the troubled are human
even in the depth of their illness, and long and need to feel
loved rather than abandoned.

Millen Brand in the thirties wrote the novel, *The Outward Room*, describing the first attempts to apply analytic
techniques to psychosis. Mary Jane Ward in *The Snake
Pit* (scripted for motion pictures by Millen Brand and Frank
Partos), Harold Main in *If a Man Be Mad*, Paul Hackett in
The Cardboard Giants, and Fritz Peters in *The World Next
Door*, are among others who dared write about feelings and
thoughts that once threatened to destroy them. They are helping to draw attention to the great and grave national problem
of our mental hospitals.

The severely troubled, or psychotic, fall into two main
categories—schizophrenia and manic-depressive psychosis.

In schizophrenia—a word coined by Dr. Eugen Blueler to describe the "split" in the personality that seems to occur— the person withdraws into himself. The manic-depressive goes through cycles that vary in intensity, ranging from depression to elation. He may have stable periods between the swings.

Psychiatrists tell us that schizophrenics often display the symptoms of manic-depressives and vice-versa. One person may show all the symptoms in the book, or some at different times or different ones in varying degree.

Categories are apt to be overlapping, misleading, meaningless. We would be taking a big step forward if we scrapped categories and instead substituted as diagnosis: "Lack of love."

For instance, on the records of someone in a mental hospital, in place of the usual technical terminology, might be noted: "He did not receive as much love from his parents as his brother, who did not become seriously troubled. He is in need of love and skilled help from a psychiatrist."

We would take another large step forward if we could think of the severely troubled not as "mentally ill" but "emotionally ill." There is nothing wrong with the minds of many we label "mentally ill." It is their emotions that are disturbed.

What's in a name? Plenty, when it is used to perpetuate hopelessness and apathy. Those who do not know therapeutic love sometimes sing the refrain, "Psychotics cannot be helped." But a number *have* been helped by wise, skilled analysts and have lost their "psychotic" traits, which turn out to be defenses at feeling unloved.

[180]

There are a larger number of the troubled in our mental hospitals today than ever before. But this does not necessarily mean emotional illness is on the rise.

We have more people in the nation. They live longer. We recognize emotional illness earlier. Our mental hospitals are more available. The number of those who enter voluntarily is growing. The mental hospitals are housing many of the aged who are not emotionally ill but who are there because they have no other place to go. These are among the reasons responsible for the increase.

We pay more today for the care of our severely troubled although what we give is still too small for adequate care—the national average is $2.12 a day per person.

Our mental hospitals, on the whole, are in poor physical shape, overcrowded and understaffed. *The Shame of the States* is the title Albert Deutsch gave his book which graphically describes conditions in a number of them.

Some hospitals report fifty to eighty per cent above capacity. To the question, "Do mental hospitals railroad anyone?" a superintendent laughed bitterly and replied: "We haven't even got the space to take care of those we know need help. We want people to *leave,* not enter."

Asked what words came to mind if he were to describe the physical condition of the nation's mental hospitals, Dr. J. R. McGibony, in charge of hospital construction for the United States Public Health Service, answered: "Several words come to mind but they're not fit to say in the presence of a lady."

Not only do the old buildings make living uncomfortable

for the troubled and the men and women who take care of them, but some are literal death traps. A recent fire in a West Virginia mental hospital killed seventeen. "I know it's too late to say this, but we submitted to the budget director a recommendation for $1,000,000 for fireproofing our institution," the supervisor of the West Virginia state institutions told the newspapers.

Shortage of staff is put at 65 per cent. We need, according to American Psychiatric Association standards, 14,500 more psychiatric nurses, 3,400 more psychiatric social workers, 2,000 more psychiatrists and 250 more clinical psychologists.

The number of psychiatrists needed by the hospitals is, at best, a vague guess. No one really knows. It depends on whom you ask and what kind of help they advocate. Some estimates go as high as 10,000.

There are only two psychiatrists for 800 patients in a leading New York state hospital. One woman, supposedly getting intensive help, has seen a psychiatrist only eleven times during the past year, from thirty to forty-five minutes each session. Most patients do not see a psychiatrist this often. Bryce Hospital, Alabama, has one psychiatrist for every 1,100 patients. Throughout the country the average is one for every 400 to 500.

Our ostrich approach is responsible for tragedies such as suicides and murders committed by those who have been in institutions where they have received little or no help, either while there or after leaving. Mental hospitals try to screen the troubled thoroughly before letting them go home, but cannot possibly insure against danger because the odds are so high.

"As long as it's true that we have one psychiatrist for every 400 to 500 patients, we're likely to have occasional crimes of violence committed by former inmates," said Dr. Felix. "The burden is beyond what an individual should be expected to carry, especially if he is dealing with the delicate task of releasing patients."

He reported what every psychiatrist knows:

There is not one public mental hospital in the country with enough staff, nor one adequate program to help the troubled after they leave, nor one adequate out-patient clinic program where the troubled who have or have not been hospitalized can go for periodic check-ups.

We do not have enough psychiatrists to staff mental hospitals. We are not paying enough to the ones we have. We are not training enough to meet immediate, let alone future needs. We do not possess enough facilities to take care of the less troubled.

But the picture is not all grim. We are starting in small ways to face the problem of mass inner terror.

Dr. Felix's organization, the National Mental Health Institute, represents an official beginning. As taxpayers, we allocate to it $11,000,000 annually to conduct our national war against mental illness. It distributes funds for training, conducts research, and financially helps states set up services.

But this is not much money compared to the $30,000,000 spent in 1947, for example, by the Department of Agriculture, to eradicate foot and mouth disease in animals. Or when we remember that each one whose emotional illness has been halted represents a saving of $100,000 to the taxpayer, according to Dr. Karl Menninger.

Mental illness strikes down seven times as many persons in the productive years of their lives as cancer, yet we spend only one-seventh as much on research for mental illness as on cancer. (690 persons require hospitalization for emotional illness to every 100 cancer patients, between the ages of 25 and 34). There is growing belief, too, that cancer is related to emotional disturbances, that it is one of the ways the body may fight to solve psychological problems.

Only two cents is spent on psychiatric research in this country for every $50 on industrial research and every $100 on medical research. We need the research, but perhaps we need even more the training of those skilled in the art of helping the troubled.

Some believe this is the first need, that we can research to our heart's content but it will not help the troubled feel better.

"Those who must still do 'research' on why men become emotionally ill, lack conviction about the cause of emotional illness," declared a leading psychiatrist. "Men become emotionally ill, for the most part, because they were denied love as children. We need more men and women who can give the troubled a feeling of being loved and accepted so they can face their fear."

Money is needed, but not money alone. Also needed are men of vision—like those responsible for turning one state mental hospital, formerly rated as inferior, into one of the best. This happened in Topeka. Reporters walked through the yellow limestone buildings of Topeka State Hospital, saw that in spite of the old structures, the warm feeling that existed between patients and staff was helping the troubled.

They understood what Dr. Karl Menninger meant when he said earlier in the day, "The influence exerted on the patient by those who care for him is the most important medicine he can receive."

One reason for the change in the hospital, according to Dr. L. P. Ristine, superintendent, has been the cooperation between the state and a private organization—the Menninger Foundation—located down the road from the hospital. Most of the hospital's medical staff trained at the Foundation.

Dr. Menninger said, in discussing the work in the back wards of Topeka done by one psychiatrist, Dr. James M. Mott, Jr.: "An outstanding challenge both to science and to hospital administration exists in the large number of custodial cases filling up our state and federal psychiatric hospitals. There is a long tradition of pessimism regarding the recovery of patients who have been hospitalized more than three years. This pessimistic attitude becomes reinforced by reflection from doctor to relative to patient, and the other way round.

"Doctors give up trying to help patients, patients give up trying to get well, relatives give up trying to help them get well. The introduction of the new spirit of optimism can sometimes reverse this vicious cycle. We could better assume that all of our patients will get well, and expect exceptions, than to assume that most of them will not get well and be surprised at the exceptions. What is now the exception might conceivably become the rule if we could determine just what therapeutic leaven is needed in each particular case.

"This is the philosophy of many contemporary psychiatrists, and it is contrary to the malignant pessimism of past years."

Dr. Mott worked with men and women hospitalized for many years. One 72-year-old woman, there for seventeen years, had lived in constant fear of a gang of criminals plotting to kill her. Dr. Mott talked to her daily. She gradually lost her hallucinations and was able to work in the community as a housekeeper while she continued to visit him weekly for further help.

An example of imagination was shown in New Jersey. The state mental hospital at Trenton suffered a shortage of help at the same time that the women's prison at Clinton Farms was overcrowded. Dr. F. Lovell Bixby, deputy commissioner in charge of correction and parole for the state, hearing the plea of Edna Mahan, superintendent of the women's prison, that something be done to house the extra prisoners, suddenly thought of a novel idea.

Why not let a selected group of women prisoners, under careful supervision, care for the 660 severely troubled women housed at the Mercer Field unit of Trenton State Hospital, a former air station turned over by the Navy to the state for mental hospital patients? The unit had extra room for the prisoners.

He consulted Dr. Edward Humphreys, former deputy commissioner in charge of mental institutions, and Commissioner

Sanford E. Bates, head of the state's Department of Institutions and Agencies, both men of vision. They agreed the plan was worth trying.

It worked out to everyone's benefit. A bond of sympathy developed between many of the prisoners and patients.

One prisoner said, "You get along well with the women if you don't abuse them. Seems like they've been through enough abuse."

Another remarked, "They don't speak my language and I don't speak theirs but we make out fine if I'm gentle."

Also in the realm of wise exploration is group therapy for the severely troubled. This is used, for example, in all of the mental hospitals in New York state where emotional illness is a larger problem, numerically speaking, than in any other state. Mental Hygiene Commissioner Newton Bigelow has pushed forward this program.

Such experiments show that the wall of fear which separates the very troubled from the rest of us is slowly being broken down.

The training of psychiatric aides and psychiatric nurses, the use of volunteers in mental hospitals, the expansion of home care, the increasing number who enter mental hospitals voluntarily—these, too, tell of gains.

As does a greater interest shown by some of the public. The Masons, for example, have given $1,000,000 in the last eighteen years for research into the causes of schizophrenia. They expect to allot another $1,000,000 in the next ten years. This interest is due primarily to the leadership of an 80-year-old retired Boston lawyer, Melvin Johnson, Sovereign Grand

Commander of the Supreme Council, 33rd Degree Ancient Accepted Scottish Rite of Freemasonry, Northern Jurisdiction, U.S.A.

An increasing number of men and women donate time and dollars to the care of the troubled, either as board members or contributors to mental health organizations and institutions. There are names like Mrs. Albert Lasker, whom the nation knows well, and names that the nation will never know, like the John Smiths who help raise a few dollars for the clinic downtown.

Then there are the citizen groups working to improve conditions in mental hospitals by requesting states to spend more money. Former patients have formed organizations to help each other out as well as to work to better the hospitals.

Progress appears slow because there is such a long way to go. Not enough of us believe severely troubled are no different from anyone else except they live in greater fear, the quantity of fear also affecting the quality of their living.

The characteristics associated with the psychotic are normal if not made grotesque through fear—all of us possess, to a certain extent, what exists in any one of us.

If we accepted this, we would not show only superficial concern when an underpaid, overworked brutal attendant murders a patient or when a former patient kills an innocent bystander. We would hold a deep consistent concern, leading us to provide the compassionate care which would prevent these tragedies from occurring.

We cannot separate the problems in our back wards from the problems in our back yards. The way we feel about the very troubled in mental hospitals tells us the way we feel about ourselves. If we fear to help them, we fear to help ourselves.

As yet, we are still too afraid to help them. We fear the screams that burst from behind barred windows because they set off the screams inside ourselves. We are too busy protecting ourselves against the fear of what, to us, represents one of the most dreadful fates to befall a man—loss of one's mind.

But until we face our fear, the problem of mental illness has no solution.

CHAPTER 13

There Is No Magic

A YOUNG man rushed into a psychiatrist's office, demanded wildly, "Where can I buy a revolver?"

"Why do you want a revolver?" the psychiatrist asked.

"To kill Dr. Goode," said the young man.

The psychiatrist realized that, in coming to him, the young man was unconsciously appealing for help. Otherwise, he would have merely gone out and bought a gun. The psychiatrist called the nearest state hospital and arranged for the young man to be admitted.

At the hospital the psychiatrist who examined him asked, "Why did you want to shoot Dr. Goode?"

"Evil forces are destroying me," the young man said.

"What does Dr. Goode have to do with them?" asked the psychiatrist.

"I was walking down the street when suddenly I saw a sign advertising Dr. Goode," explained the young man. "By shooting good, I can escape the evil that is after me."

In his fearful mind, "good" and "evil" were confused. He may, in a sense, have been protesting the "good" forced on him all his life ("Be good, be good, be good"). By shooting "Dr. Goode," he may have thought he would get rid of evil.

The psychiatrist, faced with a tremendous number of patients needing him, decided neither he nor others of the staff could take the time required to give the young man enough of a feeling of safety so he could be less troubled. He could be kept in the hospital a while, then discharged without help but it might be only months before, once again, he might want to kill an innocent man and this time might actually do so.

What was the psychiatrist to do? There was no doubt that the boy had to have some kind of help.

The psychiatrist thought about electro shock. This is a form of physical treatment in which a metallic square is placed on each side of the patient's forehead. The squares are connected with a machine that sends out an electric current, setting off a convulsive reaction. There is loss of consciousness for forty or forty-five seconds during the height of the convulsion.

The psychiatrist felt the effects of electro shock would not be lasting enough. He decided on lobotomy—a major brain operation that would destroy some of the nerve centers. It would make the young man impassive, removing the violence. (This does not always happen. Lobotomized patients have committed murders. But, generally, lobotomies leave one childlike and submissive, no harm to oneself or others.)

The lobotomy was performed. The young man was returned to his home. He attempted no further violence.

Was the psychiatrist right in his decision?

Society was protected. We cannot have innocent men struck down by sudden death at the unsteady hands of the very troubled.

But what about the young man? In a sense, his life was taken away from him. Lobotomy never leaves one the same. With the removal of violence the spark of life of which the violence is an expression also disappears. The operation destroys a quality in man that cannot be replaced.

One might argue that the young man's life would have been taken from him if he had killed Dr. Goode, or that for him to spend the rest of his days in a mental hospital meant another kind of loss of life.

But in a society where there is deep regard for the dignity of each man and an understanding of the terror that produces violence, might something else have been possible? After lobotomy, little more can be done, for brain tissue has been destroyed.

Some psychiatrists (particularly neuropsychiatrists) think people become severely troubled because something is chemically or glandularly wrong with them. They believe that only treatment of the body will help the troubled feel better.

They look for a magic formula that will catapult the unhappy into sudden happiness. They search for chemical compound or brain surgery or physical process to solve the mystery of emotional illness.

They do not ask the question, "Why should this person's body not function naturally when nature intended all bodies be natural unless something interfered?" They do not ask what that "something" is into which a person may be born which terrifies him so he will suffer in both body and mind. Many psychiatrists believe most babies are born psychically sound. It is "the emotional tampering" by parents that distorts their lives, as one put it.

Those who look for a physical solution work with the least important part of man, as far as their profession goes. Both psychiatry and psychology have as their root, "psyche," the Greek word for soul. The organically-minded psychiatrists do not reach for the soul.

Brain surgery should not be performed in the early stages of mental illness when other treatment might work, Dr. Paul Hoch, in charge of psychiatric research at the New York State Psychiatric Institute, has warned. The brain is irreversibly damaged; no later treatment can be used on a lobotomized brain.

Dr. Walter Freeman, neurologist, at the 1953 annual convention of the American Psychiatric Association, estimated that 25,000 lobotomy operations have been performed in this country since 1936, when he and a colleague performed the first one.

There are two kinds of lobotomy: prefrontal and transorbital. The prefrontal, the more serious operation, involves the opening up of the skull. In the transorbital, or "icepick" operation, a surgical instrument shaped like an icepick is inserted under the eyelid. Not as much brain tissue is destroyed.

Dr. Freeman announced at the 1949 convention of the American Psychiatric Association that he was giving up the prefrontal lobotomy because of complications that resulted from it, primarily epileptic seizures. These occurred in 20 per cent of the cases operated on, and in 47 per cent of those who had two brain operations followed by electro shock, he said. He named other complications: "personality changes in the patients resulting in inertia, rudeness, inconsiderate behavior and loss of control of the bladder."

Newspapers all over the country carried Dr. Freeman's announcement. But this has not stopped many hospitals from continuing to use a serious operation whose results are still uncertain. Dr. Freeman said, however, that he would continue the simple operation, a transorbital lobotomy, which he describes as "much less damaging to the personality." Calling lobotomy "a method of last resort," he said, in a summary of his paper prepared for the press at the 1953 meeting, "If the soul can survive death, it can surely survive lobotomy." Are we to place lobotomy in the same category as death?

One young brain surgeon, preparing to do lobotomies at a New York state mental hospital, turned to a visitor and said despairingly: "What barbarism—that we must destroy some of the human brain under the guise of helping people!" He added cynically, "But if I don't, someone else will."

The value of brain surgery and shock treatments of all

kinds—insulin, electro, metrazol and other methods that have a drastic physical effect on the human body—is under strong debate among psychiatrists themselves.

It would be amusing, were it not for the fact that human lives are involved, to hear at meetings first one psychiatrist report that shock has helped *his* patients, to be immediately contradicted by another who claims it has had a detrimental effect on *his* patients.

Dr. Lothar Kalinowski, the psychiatrist who introduced electro shock to this country from Italy, and who is now at the New York State Psychiatric Institute, has said shock is helpful in psychosis, but warned against its use "indiscriminately" in neurosis. He held that neurotics may be harmed by it, their anxiety aggravated by shock.

Nonetheless, some psychiatrists use it freely on the mildly troubled, setting up assembly line electro-shock shops. Not content with simple shock, some have devised a supercharged shock called B.E.S.T.—Blitz Electric Shock Therapy.

Does shock help troubled people feel better? The most thoughtful and comprehensive study to date measuring the long-term effect of electro shock comes to us from the Royal Edinburgh Hospital for Mental and Nervous Disorders. Dr. Shafica Karagulla reports on 923 patients studied for eighteen years. The survey is based on the illness for which electro shock is considered most effective—manic-depressive psychosis. It is used for depressive states; insulin coma is generally preferred for schizophrenia.

This is believed to be the first report to include a complete follow-up of troubled people after shock, throughout hospitalizations and remissions. Usually reports discuss only a small number of cases and lack details on what happens in the years following.

Dr. Karagulla's conclusion: The use of electro shock does not seem to reduce the period of hospitalization "to any significant degree," nor does it decrease the duration of the illness.

Further: Those discharged as "recovered" in the group treated with shock had a higher percentage of relapse within six to twelve months after leaving the hospital than those in the control groups who were given only sedation, psychotherapy and occupational therapy.

"The percentage of patients discharged from the hospital after a depressive illness does not vary greatly whether they are treated conservatively or by E. C. T. [Electric Convulsive Therapy]," he said. "Such slight differences as may exist are statistically insignificant.

"The writer originally hoped that convulsion therapy might be proved to reduce the number of such 'chronic' patients (those who do not recover from a depressive illness) but no evidence was found to substantiate this hope," he said.

Some authorities have stressed the importance of early administration of shock as a preventive measure against chronic illness, "but again, the evidence in this survey does not support this belief," says Dr. Karagulla.

The inevitable conclusion is that shock is "palliative" rather than "curative," Dr. Karagulla said, with the chance that some are made worse by it.

Another important evaluation of shock therapy has been made by the Group for the Advancement of Psychiatry, one of the nation's leading psychiatric organizations. While shock is "of unquestioned benefit in certain psychiatric conditions," there are "widespread abuses," it reported. The abuses are listed as:

"1. Its use on non-hospitalized patients without safeguards and by unqualified persons.

"2. Its administration to patients without due regard to an adequate evaluation of the patient's personality, his problems and the potentialities of other forms of therapy.

"3. Its routine immediate use to the exclusion of adequate psychotherapy.

"4. Its use as a sole therapeutic agent to the neglect of a complete psychiatric program."

Some members of the group added an even stronger statement to the report. They felt that "under good psychiatric management," electro shock treatment was often "not necessary as a life-saving measure." Familiarity with a wide range of psychiatric therapy and practice reduced the need for its use.

Some state mental hospital authorities have remarked, after shock or lobotomy has been administered to a violent patient, "He will be more tractable now." In terms of the shortage of psychiatrists and attendants this attitude can be understood but not condoned.

Insulin, electro shock, metrazol or a combination thereof, may have the effect of quieting down a troubled person. Instead of stirring up a ward, he will contain himself. The harassed, underpaid staff have it easier, at least for a while. But it is also possible that some will become more violent, rebellious, or terrified.

Shock may cause death. A few cases of death occurred due to heart failure, according to a study of 14,000 persons given electro shock in New York state hospitals. One man developed pleurisy after a fractured rib and died.

A few patients suffered fracture of ribs and bones although the most common complication was "a biting of the tongue and lips, followed at times by dislocation of the jaw." In some instances teeth were loosened or lost. Nausea and vomiting often followed shock.

In addition to physical danger, there are psychological dangers. The psychiatrists who made the study warned that those anxious lest they lose their "sanity" through shock "frequently" became more disturbed after it.

Shock may also lead troubled people to believe they are getting something that will enable them to solve their problems. Comes the next emotional crisis and if they fail, they are often even more helpless than before because they expected to be stronger. They then think, "Even shock can't help me. I am lost."

Some psychiatrists say they use shock and surgery only after everything else has been tried.

"Everything else—except the real treatment of talking to the patient," countered one psychiatrist.

What does it feel like to undergo shock? Each one's reaction may be different. Some may become more depressed. Some may feel reborn with a new chance at life because of the temporary relief of guilt through a sense of punishment. Some may experience an unconscious feeling of death or near-death, although not certain or specific. Some may feel no effect at all.

One woman's reaction was described by Dr. Malcolm L. Hayward, of Hall-Mercer and Pennsylvania Hospitals and the Department of Psychiatry, University of Pennsylvania School of Medicine, in a paper in The Psychiatric Quarterly, published by the New York State Department of Mental Hygiene.

He told of his discussion with a twenty-year-old girl who had received thirty-four electro shock and sixty insulin shocks—totalling fifty comas. In spite of all these "treatments" she showed "little or no improvement," and was finally referred to Dr. Hayward for "direct analytic therapy," a new technique developed by Dr. John N. Rosen. After six months she was free of "committable psychosis," Dr. Hayward reported.

At one point he asked, "Joan, as you look back over all your treatment, how do you feel about E.S.T. [Electro Shock Therapy]?"

"I hated the cold thing on my forehead and the split second of jerking when I was out of control before I was unconscious," she replied. "It was like an orgasm and made me feel real terror. I hated the people who held me down."

She went on, "It's like watching a person die in the electric chair. You watch them writhe and squirm. I would watch myself. I didn't mind the others watching so much as watching myself. Only the part of you that is censor is alive during E.S.T. The physical part of you is dead and out of control. It was humiliating.

"I didn't want the insulin to cure me. I wanted it to kill me. Insulin and E.S.T. only work when the patient fears being killed."

The doctor said, "Wait a minute, now, Joan. How about the patients who ask to be killed but get better after shock?"

"Oh, they don't really want to die and stay dead," she replied. "They need punishment. They feel so guilty they think they deserve to be killed. Only by being punished can they hope to be happy again. To them 6 and 4 [agitated wards] are hell. They feel that is where they should be. The doctor seems to be God and he decrees death but then, during the killing, God decides they don't need to die entirely. Often the patients say, 'God has let me off.' "

Some mental hospitals use drugs to try to help the troubled. Sodium amytal, in certain dosage, may bring back to reality the catatonic (a type of schizophrenia characterized either by a stupor or a state of extreme excitement). This drug may also produce a semi-hypnotic effect on the less troubled, allowing them access to hidden memories. It was used during the war in cases of battle fatigue or shock. It is also used occasionally as an anaesthetic in operations because the depth of sleep can be closely controlled.

The use of sodium amytal was demonstrated at Trenton State Hospital, Trenton, New Jersey. A young man, in the stuporous catatonic state, was wheeled into the treatment ward. He lay on the cot as though dead.

Dr. Grant Johnston, a psychiatrist, raised the young man's

hand in the air. It remained upright as if it were wax or wood and no part of him.

"He has not spoken a word since he entered the hospital last week," explained Dr. Johnston.

The records showed that for the last two years the young man had acted strangely, refusing to do anything except housework. His mother said she had spoiled him as a child, petting him to get him to eat. He never cried, she recalled, not even as a baby. He had "never gone out with girls." In the week preceding his admission to the hospital, he had suddenly "gone crazy," she said. He crawled around the floor looking for "spirits" and insisting he was a snake.

The nurse wiped a patch of the boy's arm with antiseptic. Dr. Johnston deftly inserted a needle into a vein. The sodium amytal started to flow through the boy's body.

The first sound to come from him in a week was a moan. He opened his eyes and stared out the window at trees. Dr. Johnston bent over him and asked, "Do you know where you are?"

In a low voice, the young man said, "Yes."

"Where?"

"In a hospital."

"Do you know what month this is?"

As though fighting to remember, the boy answered, "October." (It was December.)

"What are you doing in a hospital?" asked Dr. Johnston.

"I don't know. A doctor put me here," the boy said slowly.

"Is anything bothering you?"

At first he did not reply. Then he said, "You got a lot of beds here."

"Have you felt upset in the last week?"

"Up—where?" The young man was confused.

"Why wouldn't you talk to us?"

"When?" He screwed up his face, trying to remember.

"A while ago."

The young man said, "I don't know."

Suddenly he started to struggle against the strip of sheet that bound his wrist to the cot. A medical student, watching the procedure, started to untie the strip on order from Dr. Johnston.

The young man struck out at the student.

"Why did you do that?" asked Dr. Robert E. Bennett, the hospital's clinical director, who had been listening to the conversation.

"He's no good," muttered the young man.

"Why is he no good?"

"He tried to poison me," the young man mumbled.

"How did he try to poison you?" asked Dr. Bennett.

"He put something on me," the young man said. Then he yawned several times, turned over on his side and closed his eyes. Sodium amytal is so relaxing it sometimes puts patients to sleep.

"I have a feeling that most of the patients are really dying to talk," said Dr. Johnston. "They are like two-year-old children lost in the dark. Some of them even tell you they feel a gray fog creeping over their brains."

Under the influence of the drug some confess feelings of

shame, guilt and hatred. They may not recall afterwards what they have said, but they appear temporarily relieved. This young man, when he awakened, might be able to talk more freely or he might relapse into his catatonic state, the hospital authorities said.

The use of drugs is another "short-cut" method that is highly debatable. Some say it helps the psychiatrists more than the patients, that if the troubled person cannot reach his unconscious consciously, living through the emotion of the unconscious thought, he is not really helped.

"The more you get to know the individual patient, the less you use shock or drugs and the more you use psychological methods," said Dr. Bennett. "If we had the time, we could use more of the psychological methods. But pressure is too great, we need the beds and we are short of psychiatrists. Also, most families want the patient back as soon as it is possible for him to leave."

Sic transit the troubled from hospital to home and from home back to hospital. And we wonder why so many enter again and again.

Some new drug or process is constantly being hailed as the miracle that will cure the severely troubled. None of the "miracle cures" have stood up, although some of the troubled seem to be helped temporarily.

This raises the point to what extent the added attention given someone may be the reason for the apparent recovery rather than anything that is done "to" him. The very fact that someone pays attention may help the troubled feel better momentarily.

[204]

We all require a certain amount and quality of attention. The severely troubled need an even greater amount because they did not get enough of the right kind as children. They need someone who will take interest in them—even a moment's interest is better than none at all.

But instead of shock and lobotomy, there is another way of helping the severely troubled, one that is proving far more effective. It represents the maximum in attention that can be paid a troubled person—psychoanalysis.

Psychoanalysis is difficult, expensive and takes a long time but, thus far, seems to be the only treatment that has really helped. In this country, the late Dr. Harry Stack Sullivan, the late Dr. Paul Federn, Dr. Frieda Fromm-Reichmann, and others have had remarkable results with it.

If trouble is a matter of degree, then what best helps the mildly troubled will best help the severely troubled, although it may have to be used more intensely and, perhaps, a little differently.

In the psychoanalysis of the severely troubled, distinction must be made between the clearing up of what is called "the psychotic episode" or break with reality, and the help that follows, explains Dr. K. R. Eissler, psychoanalyst.

Thus, there are two stages. The first helps the troubled person lose his delusions or hallucinations, and the second helps him go through the long, careful process of psychoanalysis, necessary if he is to forsake the fear which led to his illusionary world.

Because of the scarcity of analysts, it might seem practical that they work with those most easily helped rather than spend long years struggling with the very troubled. Yet, it is important that there be some who show that the very troubled can recover, for some day there may be enough time, money and energy to help a large number of them as well as to help others from becoming severely troubled.

The severely troubled need love in even greater quantity than the less troubled.

"Love in all its myriad forms still stands as the principal prescription for the treatment of schizophrenia," says Dr. Milton Wexler, lay analyst who has successfully helped the severely troubled through psychoanalytic techniques. "Affection and sympathy, tenderness and approval—these are the medicines of choice," he said. "Dosage, of course, depends on the capacity of the therapist to give."

The work of Dr. John Rosen, called "direct analysis," has attracted much attention in the profession. Some who help the severely troubled believe it takes a long time for them to feel safe enough to start the return to reality. These therapists give a gentle, slow support while they wait.

The governing principle of direct analysis is that "the therapist must be a loving, omnipotent protector and provider for the patient." Expressed another way, "he must be the idealized mother who now has the responsibility of bringing the patient up all over again." (This, too, is what others who work with the severely troubled believe.)

But Dr. Rosen takes a more active part. He talks directly to the troubled person's unconscious. He explains:

"Direct interpretations differ significantly from the interpretations used in the analysis of the neurotic. Interpretations are made to the neurotic patient after he has learned from his therapist the meaning of symbols, dream interpretations, the associative logic of slips of the tongue and the affective consequence of the transference. Direct analysis does not require this preparation before making interpretations. It is as though the psychotic already knows what the neurotic goes to such pains to find out. The psychotic seems just about to know what the unconscious ego has been doing and why it has been doing it, and this preparation causes the patient to absorb the meaning of the interpretations as though there were no resistances.

"The direct interpretation relates to the governing principle because it lets the sufferer know that his mumbo jumbo signals, like those used by the infant, are being understood."

Other analysts have independently developed such techniques with very troubled children. Dr. Rosen is believed to be the first one to use them with severely disturbed adults.

To give an example of how Dr. Rosen works, here in part is his description of one patient. Joan, twenty-five-year-old mother of two children, was brought to his office in a very disturbed condition. She wore a dirty housedress and sneakers and her long hair streamed untidily down her back. She talked unceasingly in a rapid monotone, punctuated by gasps, tears and laughter, except when she was quietly preoccupied with some "magical act."

During the first few visits Dr. Rosen listened carefully to her. He told her he was there to protect her and would not let her hurt herself or others. At one point she crawled through the door in his office on her hands and knees. Another time she started struggling violently with him when he tried to keep her in the room.

"I told Joan several times that I was going to protect her, but that I also had to control her," he said. "I ordered her to lie still. She did finally, and I asked her why she fought me when I loved her and protected her. She put her left thumb in her mouth and sucked it vigorously saying, 'Ooh, that's good. That's wonderful. I want it again and again.' Then she removed this thumb and sucked on her right thumb."

The following dialogue ensued:

Patient: Out, out. He says to take the thumb out. Take it out.

Doctor: You have me mixed up with your mother. Did she tell you not to put your thumb in your mouth? (Patient nods.) Were you a thumb sucker as a baby? (Patient nods.) I don't mind if you suck your thumb.

Patient: Thank goodness.

Doctor: That's all right. Don't bite it. You can keep it there as long as you want. It's all right. It's all right. Do you get pleasure from it?

Patient: Yes.

Doctor: Is it very exciting?

Patient: Yes. Yes. Hard. Hard. Hard. I love them. Christ, I love cigarettes. Why doesn't someone give me a taste, a taste. I want my thumb. I want my thumb. I can't have my thumb. It's nice to suck a thumb. A baby can certainly suck a thumb with its mother.

Doctor: I am your mother now and I will permit you to do whatever you want.

Patient: (Sucks thumb vigorously, breathing deeply and regularly).

Dr. Rosen first appeared to Joan like her depriving mother must have seemed to her as a child. When he granted her permission to suck her thumb, he became the good parent.

It is necessary for the therapist to win all struggles with the patient, Dr. Rosen believes. He says: "The therapist is the forbidding parent. The patient hates the forbidding parent and wishes him dead. If the patient succeeds in this magical disposing of the forbidding parent, he himself is lost. Picture an infant at the breast level. Imagine it alone in the midst of a forest in deepest Africa. As far as the neo-natal infant knows, this might well be so because there is no one other than himself and his breast-mother as yet in his object world. If the parent is destroyed, what will happen to the infant?"

Dr. Rosen also warns that it is not enough merely to bring someone back to reality. It is then necessary to follow this with the usual psychoanalytic procedure to safeguard the gains of the previous therapy.

Some analysts approve, others disapprove of Dr. Rosen's technique. Some say more time must be allowed to elapse to see whether his treatment is successful.

But no matter what the arguments are for or against him, Dr. Rosen has added dramatically to the proof provided by a number of analysts that there is a way other than shock or surgery to help the severely troubled.

It is a way that costs more but how much is a life worth? We give money to fight for survival through guns and atom bombs, but we do not give money to fight for survival in other, more lasting ways.

It is understandable that superintendents of mental hospitals, overwhelmed by large numbers of the very troubled and possessing small numbers of men and women to care for them, feel helpless. They are apt to try any treatment they think might ease pain, believing this better than nothing.

The question is: "May it not be wiser to do nothing than do something that is, perhaps, little good in the long run, and which might harm?"

We have to ask ourselves this, as a nation, when we condone countless brain operations and shock treatments for our very troubled. We have to ask if we are not, as in our individual lives, accepting the easy way because we will not pay, both in money and psychological investment, for a better and harder way.

Dr. Robert Lindner, lay analyst, attacks what he calls "the twin abortions" of psychiatry—"the monstrosities of the so-called convulsive or shock therapies and their rival miscreation, psychosurgery."

"Both of these take their cue from the idea—never admitted, needless to say—that if one cannot or will not adjust by himself, or is recalcitrant to the persuasive adjustive techniques of the other forms of treatment and persists in his maladjustive behavior and thoughts—then, by God, a way must be found to pummel, pound or otherwise enforce his adjustment in spite of himself."

He says that "in effect, there is little difference between the white-coated psychiatric shock specialist and his primitive forebear, the mud-daubed witch doctor, who also treated diseases of the mind by scaring out, shaking out, routing out, and exorcising by dire agony and inhuman ordeal the demons or devils—today disguised by scientific sounding names —which they believed caused patients to behave in such deplorable, tactless or irritating ways."

Those who perform surgery and give electro shock say they are relieving human suffering even if only temporarily, and that the relief is important. But others insist there is a better way, a more humane way, and a way that may be lasting.

When we settle for anything less than the best, we are still asking for magic, just like our ancestors in the jungle. The demand for a quick solution to emotional illness is the demand for some mystical formula that will recreate quickly what it has taken years to destroy.

In our desire for relief of suffering, we are prone to accept any way out of pain, preferring temporary relief rather than paying the higher price of a more lasting way out.

There may be no easy answer to the problem of mental illness and anyone looking for it may be doomed to disappointment. When one has become severely troubled, one may have to work hard over a long time to regain health.

Surgery, shock, injections, all do things *to* a person from the outside. Psychoanalytic techniques reach inside him, altering for the better the whole desperate, conflicted inner balance (or unbalance) of the emotions. This gives him more awareness of the self and the world around him.

In the neurotic as well as in the second phase of treating the psychotic, when psychoanalysis may be used, deep change does not occur unless one takes part in it and helps himself.

"What is needed for real change is that emotional insight which stirs us to the very depths of our being, and which tells us: 'I am no longer doomed by what others once did to me, if I can feel and understand, *now*, what *I myself* am doing to my real self and to others," as Dr. Frederick A. Weiss, psychoanalyst, has put it.

Hypnosis, narco-analysis, shock therapy, only diminish this awareness of self, he holds. "Indeed, a kind of *shock therapy* is needed. But this need, in by far the most of the 'neurotic personalities of our time,' is not for any shock treatment which by physical or chemical means *lessens* the awareness of our human feelings. Rather, it is for *that deep, emotional shock* through which our innermost human nature is powerfully *made aware*, both of our present inhumanity and of our inherent potentiality—and responsibility—to become human. Then, human nature can change."

When what is wrong with someone is caused by his childhood fear of parents whom he believed veritable Titans of terror, electric or chemical shock can do nothing, at best, but temporarily hurl him back into painful reality without changing his feelings about himself or the world.

The only way out of emotional illness is to gain true knowledge of the self. We do not have enough competent psychiatrists or analysts to help the severely troubled know themselves. The choice facing mental hospitals, at present, is whether to give deep help to only a few or palliative help to many.

Just as, with an individual, it may be better when in doubt to take a deep breath and wait, so with our severely troubled it may be better to wait and consider with wisdom what we really want for them.

Statistics are meaningless when a hospital reports that so many thousands of patients have been discharged in the past year, an increase of so much per cent over the year before. We must ask:

How many have been in before and how many times?

How many will be back and how soon?

Discharged to what—the same life that caused torment in the first place?

What has the hospital done besides giving a jolt which may have removed some symptoms temporarily?

What do we call "treatment"?

The realistic picture is that thousands suffer so deeply from emotional illness that, under present state mental hospital conditions, most of them probably will not recover unless they do so spontaneously.

Is it right to shock or stun into submission thousands of the troubled, even those with a chance of recovery, rather than spend the time and money for better methods of treatment? Each one of us—hospital administrator, psychiatrist, taxpayer —must answer this for himself.

"We have but scratched the surface of the human soul," Dr. Brill once said.

Compassionate care for the very troubled helps us delve beneath that surface, benefiting all mankind. The more we ease the pain of those who suffer deeply, the more we understand what goes on in ourselves.

We pay a steep price for the easy way out. We must know, in the long run, that it is less expensive, psychologically and financially, to accept what has proven most effective in easing the troubled mind. We should ignore all synthetic panaceas.

CHAPTER 14

The Break in the Chain

"**W**HY wasn't something done earlier?"
This cry echoes whenever man's misery suddenly explodes. We must still wait for tragedy to blast us out of lethargy.

Statistics show a rise in divorce, delinquency, alcoholism, drug addiction, death from accidents, suicides, murders and the number of hospitalized mentally and physically ill. But all statistics really say is that people are more troubled.

[215]

Each criminal, if his life is searched, leaves clues that lead to the crime he will commit. After the deed, reporters have no difficulty unearthing a past that points to the coming destruction. They usually find his childhood life one of psychic or physical brutality, or both.

"Couldn't someone have prevented the crime?" we ask.

Yes, someone who could look deep into a child's heart and know the agony there.

When a prominent government official killed himself recently, there were those who wondered, "How could a successful man like that commit suicide?" But those who were close to him knew he had lived for years tormented by troubled feelings.

Trouble shows its cards well ahead of the play. Those who wish to see can observe the shadows cast in advance of suffering.

Troubled feelings grow more intense over the years. The lame become lamer, the halt more halt and the blind, blinder. The theory that trouble takes care of itself is fallacious. Trouble takes care of itself by promoting itself.

We do not stand still emotionally speaking. We move forward or backward. And although the moves may be imperceptible, they slowly add up either to happiness or unhappiness.

A psychic stitch in time may save more than nine. It may save a life. For the troubled die needlessly because they cannot seek help or because they cannot get help.

They slip on banana peels, fall in bathtubs, cut themselves with knives, crash in cars—100,000 a year end their lives.

It is no accident that some are accident-prone. Studies show that those who get in one accident after another are among the troubled. Our unconscious is designed to help protect us against accidents, along with our conscious. But the unconscious of a troubled man, busy fighting phantoms of the past, may not be free enough to help warn him against a car speeding down on him, or allow him to see quickly enough a sharp object over which he may stumble.

Accidental deaths account for the loss of more working years than any other cause of death, according to a study, "What Is the Leading Cause of Death?" by Frank G. Dickinson, director, and Everett L. Welker, associate in mathematics, of the Bureau of Medical Economic Research of the American Medical Association. What percentage of these accidental deaths are caused by the unconscious we do not know, but psychoanalysts believe it to be high.

The troubled die at their own hands—20,000 a year—and 100,000 more make an attempt to take their lives. One man wrote recently to a friend: "I have felt so desperate so much of my life. I now find I have reached a point where, unless I can talk to someone who cares whether I live or die, I will take my life."

He was able to describe how he felt. Some can never bring themselves to talk of death and no one knows of their despair until the suicide note is opened with its inevitable, "I can go on no longer."

Thousands of others die because men hate so deeply they must murder, even though, many times, they know not whom they murder.

The troubled die in other ways. They die because they postpone taking care of physical pain until an appendix ruptures or a gall bladder bursts.

Some die from overwork. They tax body and mind far beyond temperance. Those who plunge into their jobs with a passion that belongs not between man and work but between man and woman are using work to hide troubled feelings. The more desperately they work, the more troubled they are.

At the other extreme are those who hate work and they die in another way—a slow death. Some of these would like to be beachcombers, to get away, they say, from the daily grind and irritating bosses. What they really want is to escape the inner self. But the self stays with them even though they pick up seashells and a far heavier weight it is than the shells.

It is natural to want to work in moderation to feel fulfilled. Work should be to an adult as play to a child, enjoyable and satisfying. Work is torment only to those who use it to try to solve unknown conflicts. To them, not even relaxation is fun. They bring to mind Cicero's line, "He is never less at leisure than when at leisure."

The troubled die in mental institutions. Forgotten and forlorn they spend their last days on earth escaping from themselves and the world.

"Be wise today; 'tis madness to defer," said poet Edward Young in the seventeenth century.

Actual madness it may be, for one out of every sixteen of us breaks down emotionally. Those who defer wisdom too long live as haunts in our mental hospitals.

People do not suddenly "go mad." They have displayed warning signs over the years.

"The break with reality must be thought of not as a sudden and unexpected snapping, as of a twig, but as the gradual bending as well, which preceded the snapping," Dr. Robert Knight, psychoanalyst, puts it.

This bending starts in childhood. It may occur wherever the quality of madness pervades a house. The madness may not possess completely but only torture with a light touch, withdrawing, then invading, then withdrawing.

It is felt wherever children live frozen in fear, waiting for an explosion that never comes off. Or wherever screams and curses rip the air, destroying calm. Children live in dread of moments when parents lose their tempers. They are aware of the madness inherent in "getting mad." Not only are they afraid of madness in parents but they fear they, too, may be mad for daring to doubt the sanity of the ones to whom their lives are entrusted. They live in terror of madness and in terror of being killed, for a madman may kill if he loses enough control.

If we can help the children who live in the shade of madness we will prevent them from going over into darkness. We may save them, their children and their children's children from inner terror.

In all ways possible we should help children who are troubled and who cannot speak for themselves. For it is the children who, in large part, will shape the world's future. If they can be happier, the world will be happier. If they dwell in anger, the world will be angry.

We now know that those who are troubled lack love and, in their fear may hurt themselves and others, sometimes unto death. We have only to put this knowledge to use.

By getting help when they need it, parents may save themselves and their children much unhappiness. By knowing what went wrong in their lives, they may be able to prevent this wrong from being perpetuated on their children.

Every parent wants to love his child. When he cannot give love, it is because of his unconscious feelings. Children must feel an unconscious as well as conscious love in order to survive psychologically. The best instruction in mental hygiene principles on how to handle children is of little avail if a parent's unconscious needs are so destructive he must vent them on his child.

"Why are so many parents unable to enjoy their children?" asks Dr. Benjamin Spock, a leading child care authority.

Because they are unable to enjoy themselves. If they could feel good about themselves, they would enjoy their children, for they displace on children their feelings about themselves.

"My mother hates me," one little girl insisted to a psychoanalyst.

"She doesn't hate *you*, she just hates everything—primarily herself," the analyst said.

The child is "vulnerable, terribly vulnerable," to the attitudes of parents, warns Dr. Spock.

"If he is regularly shamed for his accidents, he acquires a sense of shame and unworthiness. If he is excessively dominated, he becomes defiant or submissive. If he is constantly warned that the parent will no longer love him unless he behaves differently, his whole personality will be poisoned with uneasiness and antagonism," he told the 1950 White House Conference on Children and Youth.

Some parents pay too much attention to children and spoil them ("Spoil," according to Webster, means "to impair seriously, vitiate, mar, ruin"). Others pay too little attention and neglect them. ("Neglect," says Webster, means "to be remiss in attending to, fail to do, care for.") Either extreme may feel like psychological murder to a child because neither stems from love.

Our schools can also save children distress by recognizing the ones who are troubled. It is not only the disobedient, delinquent pupil who may need help but the withdrawn, quiet one who seldom talks, or the very aggressive child inwardly driven to beat out all others scholastically or athletically.

Both public and private schools have responsibility. A boy attending an exclusive boarding school may face just as poignant problems as a boy in a public school in the slums.

We may well ask what price intellectual maturity without emotional maturity? The youth of the nation seem to learn about almost everything except the most important thing in life—themselves.

"Children learn to bound the States of the Union and they memorize the names and dates of bygone wars; they study the habits of beavers, learn about the distant stars, and the antics of Mother Goose, but the subject of human behavior, human motives and the inner life of man has been pretty much ignored in schools," says Dr. Arthur T. Jersild, psychologist and educator.

The three R's no longer are enough if we want to bring up a nation of emotionally healthy children. First, we must help those who feel troubled so they will not become more troubled. We must keep others from becoming troubled.

Among the children who may need help are the 6,000,000 whose families are disrupted by divorce, death or desertion; the 1,900,000 who suffer from chronic disease or physical impairment, and the 100,000 born out of wedlock.

Each year 1,000,000 children are taken into custody by the police. These are our so-called "delinquents" whom we still feel we must punish, not help.

Punishment does not fit crime. Punishment helps neither the one who gives nor the one who receives. Those who rebel resent even more a world that serves up hate when they need love. This merely increases the fear and anger already so intense within them they cannot care enough about themselves or society to respect its laws.

The cost to the child in terms of suffering should be our first concern. But we should also care about the expense to ourselves as taxpayers. The delay in getting proper help to children means that in years ahead they will fill our general hospitals, courts, welfare rolls, prisons, mental hospitals—costing us billions of dollars of needless expenditures.

We possess a penny-wise, pound-foolish philosophy. It would cost more to give help now, but in the long run it would cost far less. We will pay a high price in the years to come for not using our heads now.

For example, of the 150,000 troubled persons committed to mental hospitals each year, twenty-five per cent are under eighteen, which means they have felt severely troubled early in life. Because they did not receive help when they first needed it, we will pay for the care of a large number who will spend the rest of their lives in mental hospitals.

There are today 1,000,000 children so troubled that many will eventually find their way to mental hospitals or penal institutions. Only 1,500 of them are receiving the kind of help that has proven effective, according to the Child Welfare League of America.

The severely troubled child can be helped, as a number of places are proving. The progress made by one very troubled boy, diagnosed as schizophrenic, was described by Dr. Abraham A. Fabian, psychiatric director of the Brooklyn Juvenile Guidance Center in Brooklyn, New York, at an annual meeting of the American Orthopsychiatric Association.

The boy, five years old, was brought to the center for treatment on an out-patient basis. This is a new development, allowing the child to live at home and visit the clinic for help. Usually such children have been placed in institutions.

When first seen, the boy sat in the waiting room, making faces, rocking himself and singing in a high-pitched voice. He would not talk except to repeat words mechanically.

For some unknown reason he was frightened by what he called "butterflies." He clung to his mother "like an extra appendage" and would not permit her to talk with anyone. He was terrified of strangers.

It took months before the boy would allow even momentary separation from his mother. Help was given in her presence. It consisted of the analyst taking part with the boy in games, painting and play-acting.

But meanwhile he seemed to be feeling better. He welcomed a young cousin, whom he previously disliked, as an overnight guest. He talked on the telephone. He went visiting with his father. He started to talk logically and spoke constantly about the analyst.

His mother, by this time also receiving help, gave the clue to the "butterflies" that so terrified her son. She recalled that when he was younger, she sometimes locked him in his room at night. The analyst asked the boy about this.

"They scared me—those lights," said the boy. "They seemed to be coming through the window like big butterflies. I thought they would eat me."

The "butterflies" were automobile lights flashing through Venetian blinds. They brought panic into the heart of a frightened little boy, locked in a room because he thought his mother hated him.

The analyst talked to him about the lights, discussing "shadow and substance" until he learned the difference. The boy gradually lost his fear of "butterflies."

Dr. Fabian reported that, after three years of help, he was "hardly recognizable as the vegetating, bizarre boy we first met." He was in third grade, he played with other children and seemed to enjoy being alive.

The theory that schizophrenia in children may be a defense against a powerful urge to kill, was advanced in a report given at another annual meeting of the American Ortho-psychiatric Association by Dr. Hyman Spotnitz, psycho-analyst, and Dr. Leo Nagelberg, clinical psychologist.

"The schizophrenic child—unknown to himself—appears to be a highly social being who is willing to sacrifice his own ego to protect his parents from destruction by himself," they said, describing the analytic therapy of five schizophrenic children, part of a research project at the Child Guidance Institute, Jewish Board of Guardians, New York.

They found that "the lack of emotion, the disorganization, the withdrawal from contact with other human beings, the attacks on their own egos appear to be aimed primarily at preventing the release into action of murderous impulses to-ward their parents." The children attempted to control their murderous behavior by developing a state of "not feeling" their impulses so they did not have to act on them, the au-thors said. This was their attempt "to destroy feelings which might lead to dangerous action."

In other words, these children turned destruction inward, as they repressed the desire to hit out at others. With help, all the children slowly started to feel safe enough to express their anger and eventually lost the symptoms of schizo-phrenia.

Dr. Spotnitz has observed in twenty years of helping the troubled that psychosis may be used to preserve the self.

A provocative remark may be enough to bring out a tem-porary psychotic state in a person, he said. Occasionally some may relapse into psychosis during treatment in or-der to protect the psychiatrist. One woman told him after he had said something very frank to her: "I would have killed you if I had not blacked out." The "blacking-out" was preferable to carrying out the impulse to kill.

Psychosis represents the lesser of two evils. Schizophrenia may be compared to "a frozen state in which people place themselves to survive, like a psychic deep-freeze," as novelist Millen Brand described it.

The staff of the Hawthorne-Cedar Knolls School in Hawthorne, N.Y., internationally known for its treatment of troubled children, presented the case of a schizophrenic girl at an annual meeting of the orthopsychiatric group.

"We are, in a sense, going to try to defy custom today," explained Norman V. Lourie, then director of the school. "We are going to share with you our struggles, our bewilderment and our questioning as we discuss thirteen-year-old Helen."

She had been sent to the school by Bellevue Hospital's psychiatric department which diagnosed her as "an incipient schizophrenic." Her history was one of quarrels and temper tantrums at school and at home. She scratched furniture, tore up her clothes, fought with her mother, and refused to wash herself. Her father beat her with a strap when she would not behave.

Hawthorne placed Helen in a cottage where she lived with cottage parents and other girls. She went to school, and at the same time received emotional help. Two years of this produced a different girl. She made friends, did not lose her temper, washed regularly.

A psychiatrist from Bellevue paid tribute to Hawthorne.

"I saw Helen when she was at Bellevue," he said. "We thought she was psychotic and could never get along outside a state hospital."

Some children need long, intensive help. But many need only a little. And, for those who need help, it is never too early to start.

One mother entered the offices of Community Service Society in New York, one of the country's best-known family service agencies, carrying her six-month-old baby. "She cries too much," she explained. "The doctor says there is nothing physically wrong with her. I want to know what I do that makes her cry."

It developed she was an uncertain, nervous young mother. She was not sure she wanted a baby. The baby had sensed her uneasiness and doubt, as all babies do, and was showing its unhappiness.

With help, the young woman started to feel better about her role as a mother. She enjoyed the baby more. The baby cried less. This mother's awareness that something inside herself was hurting the child saved herself and her baby immeasurable unhappiness. She broke the chain that had stretched across generations by wanting to know the cause of her baby's constant crying. She had the courage to ask "Why?"

A man in analysis was describing how he flew into a temper tantrum at the slightest frustration.

"My father always did that, too," he recalled.

Then he added thoughtfully, "This could go on forever, couldn't it, handed down from father to son. Someone has to stop this useless, tortuous pattern. I guess it's up to me to do it for my family."

If each troubled person felt this way, the children of the future would have a far greater chance for happiness. Instead, some say it's normal to be neurotic. They try to reassure themselves with the thought that they are no unhappier than the next person.

The "be glad you're neurotic" rationalization is misleading and destructive—a psychic sedative. Be glad you're neurotic instead of psychotic, if that be your choice. But it would seem wiser to regret you're neurotic and take steps to feel less troubled.

Unhappiness increases if help is neglected. Those who have not married may become more firmly entrenched behind the barricade of loneliness. Those who drink, take sleeping pills or overeat, as they find that drink, pills and food do not ease misery, will consume even more in the vain hope of escaping self.

The impatient become more impatient, running faster and faster to keep up with they know not what. The fatigued become more fatigued, drawing on conscious and unconscious reserves to fight battles that are endless because the enemy is unknown.

Some scorn help, insisting they can go it alone. But they do not go it alone. Sharp shadows of despair and desperation march by their side.

Some say they cannot afford help. Most men, if they want help earnestly enough, will find a way to pay for it. They will work extra hours or they will go to a clinic where help is available at low cost.

There are those who want help and, with a little urging would seek it, but no one takes their plea seriously.

"Oh, there's nothing wrong with you—you just *think* you're troubled," they are told.

If a person thinks he is troubled, he is. The untroubled know they do not need help.

Some authorities believe that anyone who reads about emotional problems is asking for help, either consciously or unconsciously. He may be unable to request it outright but he hoists the signals. Only the troubled will bother to find out how to feel less troubled.

Not everyone who needs it can be helped. It is unreasonable to assume they can. Some are too frightened to accept help. Like the horse led out of the burning barn, they will not take a guiding hand, but plunge back to their death.

As Dr. John C. Thurrott, psychoanalyst, said, and perhaps we must accept it, "Some will get well. Some will die. Some will remain the same—as in all nature."

But we can increase the number of those who get well. We can help the troubled know that if they do not wait until the moment when survival or doom confronts them, they will be able to save themselves.

We can help them know it is better to face hatred and discover why they feel it, than to live in hatred without ever knowing why. We can help them know that if there is hatred within, only by becoming aware of it can they turn it to love.

The task of easing trouble belongs to rich man, poor man, beggar man, thief, doctor, lawyer, Indian chief—and parent, teacher, minister, lawyer, public health nurse, psychiatrist and motorman-conductor. It belongs to all of us.

If the chains that bind us to the warlike past are to be broken, we must support wise ways of helping the troubled. We should be willing to pay for what we need—men and women who know the art and science of help.

We should accept the fact that some will not gain inner peace except through persistence and time, and others may never attain more than a small measure of it.

We should know that by reaching our troubled children we are increasing the chances of more persons to become happier with less help.

CHAPTER 15

"Know Then Thyself"

No one wants to hate if he is able to love. No one wants
to be unhappy, once convinced of a better way of living.
No one is to blame for feeling troubled.

If we are to help ourselves and others, we must first lose
our fear of troubled feelings. We must know that a man is
no more responsible for what makes him unhappy than for the
virus that causes polio. Both are beyond his control.

We cannot blame a helpless baby for being afraid because

he does not receive love. Nor can we blame parents who themselves never knew love and so cannot give what they do not know.

Instead of punishing men for their fear can we know they seek love? Can we know that they strive for gain and glory or may murder—all in a vain attempt to get love?

If we can, we will be able to help ourselves, our country and the world to greater happiness and peace.

The fight against trouble circles the globe. Not one of us stands outside it as long as nations live in fear of each other. Until no man is afraid of death from the fall of a bomb will troubled feelings cease to be everyman's province.

Peace in the world is a reflection of each man's peace of mind. Because too many are still too afraid, there is pursuit of panic, not pursuit of peace.

Men fight their inner fear with anger. War allows expression of anger, peace means giving up anger. When anger exists, men are apt to nourish it, enjoying what enhances it, regarding with mistrust and resentment whatever quiets it. They look, therefore, suspiciously at the deeds of wise men who try to bring peace, and glow with false pride at the production of monstrous machines of war.

Men should be militant when there is injustice, when they need to fight on the side that is right, but they should not hate without cause or fan hatred in others when, with the use of wisdom, they can turn that hatred to friendship.

That we help fight fear throughout the world may be a matter of our survival. Perhaps we can best do this by first easing the fear in ourselves.

It is proper that we save ourselves first. Those who save themselves first are more likely to save others. Self-appointed saviors who do not look within, but who must save the world out of their own desperate needs, may lead men to brimstone and fire.

It is right that we be happy. If we are happy, we will not put up with what is destructive and unreal, but will work to change an unhappy land, an unhappy world.

If we feel good inside ourselves, we will solve other problems with grace, for the happy are able to plan the best possible life for the greatest possible number of men. And when there are enough who are happy, the unhappy cannot stop them.

If we are happy, we will know we do not get something for nothing in this Voltairean "best of all possible worlds," and we will be willing to work for what we believe important. We will give friendship and love freely, realizing this is the easiest way in the long run. Hatred and anger, while appearing easier at the moment, impose a toll that may cost us our lives.

Above all, we should love ourselves so we may love others out of fullness, not hunger for them out of emptiness.

We should know that sex and love are to be joined in harmony, not split in fury. We should accept our body as our rightful heritage, ours to respect and enjoy, not reject or deny.

We should see ourselves as we are, not as we might wish to be. We should give up unreal ideals that add to unhappiness because they cover up inner misery; we should not settle for the outside glitter that hides pain but accept the dull sheen that is contentment.

We should know it is more important to *be* than to *do*, that what we are like matters more than what we achieve or produce. We should accept ourselves as we are, human and liable to error, and give up the illusion we must be perfect. We can then go on to fulfill all that is in us.

We should remember Alexander Pope's oft-repeated advice:

> Know then thyself, presume not God to scan;
> The proper study of mankind is man.

If we know one man—ourself—we may know all men. The understanding of self may not be easy but it holds high rewards. The denial of self may lead only to madness and destruction.

It may take strength to face the self, but once we gain that strength, it will banish the fear that has made us desperate. It will nourish the love waiting to be set free.

APPENDIX

Appendix

LIST OF STATE MENTAL HEALTH ASSOCIATIONS

Miss Gwen McWhorter, Executive Director
ALABAMA ASSOCIATION FOR MENTAL HEALTH
P.O. Box 2591
Birmingham 2, Alabama

Dr. William B. McGrath, President
ARIZONA ASSOCIATION FOR MENTAL HEALTH
Professional Building
Phoenix, Arizona

Mrs. Donald Shaskan, President
MENTAL HEALTH SOCIETY OF NO. CALIFORNIA
2015 Steiner Street
San Francisco 15, California

Mr. Chauncey A. Alexander, Executive Director
SO. CALIFORNIA SOCIETY FOR MENTAL HYGIENE
3067 West 7th Street
Los Angeles 5, California

Mr. John L. Fortson, Executive Director
CONNECTICUT ASSOCIATION FOR MENTAL HEALTH
956 Chapel Street
New Haven 10, Connecticut

Miss Editha Stone, Executive Secretary
MENTAL HEALTH ASSOCIATION OF DELAWARE, INC.
1404 Franklin Street
Wilmington 19, Delaware

Dr. Sullivan Bedell, President
FLORIDA ASSOCIATION FOR MENTAL HEALTH
2720 Park Street
Jacksonville, Florida

Mr. Luther Alverson, President
GEORGIA ASSOCIATION FOR MENTAL HEALTH
1022 Eulalia Road, N.W.
Atlanta, Georgia

Mrs. Cornelius Mulder, Executive Secretary
HAWAII SOCIETY FOR MENTAL HYGIENE
1407 Kalakaua Avenue
King-Kalakaua Building
Honolulu, Hawaii

Mrs. Martha Pitman, President
IDAHO MENTAL HEALTH ASSOCIATION
615 S. 20th Avenue
Caldwell, Idaho

Mr. Thomas J. Blakley, Executive Director
ILLINOIS SOCIETY FOR MENTAL HEALTH, INC.
123 W. Madison Street
Chicago 2, Illinois

Mr. Joseph R. Brown, Director
INDIANA ASSOCIATION FOR MENTAL HEALTH
2331 N. Meridian Street
Indianapolis 8, Indiana

Mrs. Gordon DeLay, President
IOWA SOCIETY FOR MENTAL HEALTH
314 19th Street, S.E.
Cedar Rapids, Iowa

Mrs. Helen Morrison, Secretary
KANSAS ASSOCIATION FOR MENTAL HEALTH
Masonic Temple
10th & Van Buren
Topeka, Kansas

Mr. Barry Bingham, President
KENTUCKY ASSOCIATION FOR MENTAL HEALTH
c/o The Courier-Journal
Louisville, Kentucky

Dr. Lloyd Rowland, Director
LOUISIANA SOCIETY FOR MENTAL HEALTH
816 Hibernia Bank Building
New Orleans 12, Louisiana

Mrs. Gertrude Nilsson, Executive Director
MENTAL HYGIENE SOCIETY OF MARYLAND
317 E. 25th Street
Baltimore 18, Maryland

Mrs. Irene T. Malamud, Executive Director
MASSACHUSETTS ASSOCIATION FOR MENTAL HEALTH
41 Mt. Vernon Street
Boston 8, Massachusetts

Mr. Harold G. Webster, Executive Director
MICHIGAN SOCIETY FOR MENTAL HEALTH
153 E. Elizabeth Street
Detroit 1, Michigan

Reverend George S. Siudy, President
MINNESOTA MENTAL HYGIENE SOCIETY
309 E. Franklin Avenue
Minneapolis 4, Minnesota

Mrs. James Bane, President
MISSOURI ASSOCIATION FOR MENTAL HYGIENE
1210 E. University Street
Springfield, Missouri

Mrs. Walter Needham, President
MONTANA SOCIETY FOR MENTAL HEALTH
315 Spruce Street
Anaconda, Montana

Mrs. Joy Siccardi, President
NEW JERSEY ASSOCIATION FOR MENTAL HEALTH
12 Kimball Circle
Westfield, New Jersey

Dr. Margaret Ross, Director
NEW YORK STATE SOCIETY FOR MENTAL HEALTH
105 East 22nd Street
New York 10, N. Y.

Miss Ethel Speas, Executive Secretary
NORTH CAROLINA MENTAL HYGIENE SOCIETY
P.O. Box 2599
Raleigh, North Carolina

Mr. Leonard Orvedal, President
NORTH DAKOTA MENTAL HEALTH ASSOCIATION
1006 9th Street
Bismarck, North Dakota

Mrs. Marion S. Wells, Executive Secretary
OHIO MENTAL HEALTH ASSOCIATION
503 Chamber of Commerce Building
30 E. Broad Street
Columbus 15, Ohio

Mrs. Locene Renshaw, Executive Secretary
OKLAHOMA ASSOCIATION FOR MENTAL HEALTH
P.O. Box 1672, 223½ N.W. First Street
Oklahoma City 3, Oklahoma

Mr. Melvin L. Murphy, Executive Director
MENTAL HEALTH ASSOCIATION OF OREGON
429 Park Building
Portland 5, Oregon

Mr. Herbert Clark, Associate Director
PENNSYLVANIA MENTAL HEALTH, INC.
311 S. Juniper Street
Philadelphia 7, Pennsylvania

Dr. Melvyn Johnson, President
RHODE ISLAND SOCIETY FOR MENTAL HYGIENE
100 No. Main Street
Providence, Rhode Island

Mr. Gordon Bunch, Secretary
SOUTH CAROLINA MENTAL & SOCIAL HYGIENE SOCIETY
Charleston County Health Department
Charleston, South Carolina

Mr. John C. Foster, President
SOUTH DAKOTA MENTAL HEALTH ASSOCIATION
c/o Office of the President
300 First National Bank Building
Sioux Falls, South Dakota

Mrs. Richard McNabb, President
TENNESSEE MENTAL HYGIENE SOCIETY
4175 Lyons View Pike
Knoxville, Tennessee

Mrs. Elizabeth F. Gardner, Executive Secretary
TEXAS SOCIETY FOR MENTAL HEALTH
2504 Jarratt Avenue
Austin 3, Texas

Mrs. Jane R. Wetzel, Executive Secretary
UTAH ASSOCIATION FOR MENTAL HEALTH
112 South State Street
Salt Lake City, Utah

Mr. Donald M. Eldred, President
VERMONT ASSOCIATION FOR MENTAL HEALTH, INC.
c/o Vermont State Hospital
Waterbury, Vermont

Mr. F. W. Gwaltney, Executive Secretary
MENTAL HYGIENE SOCIETY OF VIRGINIA
P.O. Box 1991, 9 No. 12th Street
Richmond 19, Virginia

Mr. George F. Ault, Executive Director
WASHINGTON ASSOCIATION FOR MENTAL HEALTH
408 Seaboard Building
Seattle 1, Washington

Mr. Walter W. Argow, Administrative and Field Director
WISCONSIN ASSOCIATION FOR MENTAL HEALTH
119 E. Washington Ave.
Madison, Wisconsin

LIST OF FEDERAL AGENCIES

NATIONAL INSTITUTE OF MENTAL HEALTH, Public Health Service, U.S. Department of Health, Education and Welfare, Bethesda 14, Maryland.

CHILDREN'S BUREAU, Mental Health Unit, U.S. Department of Health, Education and Welfare, Washington 25, D.C.

OFFICE OF EDUCATION, Exceptional Children and Youth, U.S. Department of Health, Education and Welfare, Washington 25, D.C.

OFFICE OF VOCATIONAL REHABILITATION, U.S. Department of Health, Education and Welfare, Washington 25, D.C.

LIST OF NATIONAL ORGANIZATIONS (PRIVATE)

THE NATIONAL ASSOCIATION FOR MENTAL HEALTH, INC., 1790 Broadway, New York 19, N.Y. A service agency, holds annual meeting, publishes material on all phases of mental health and two quarterly journals: *Mental Hygiene* and *Understanding the Child*. (State associations affiliated.)

NATIONAL MENTAL HEALTH COMMITTEE, 4 West 58th Street, New York 19, N.Y. Works for better mental health legislation.

AMERICAN PSYCHIATRIC ASSOCIATION, 1785 Massachusetts Avenue, N.W., Washington 6, D.C. A membership and service agency, holds annual meeting and publishes a monthly journal: *American Journal of Psychiatry*. Its program is concerned with the improvement of mental hospitals in the United States and Canada.

AMERICAN PSYCHOANALYTIC ASSOCIATION, 245-247 East 82nd Street, New York 28, N.Y. A membership agency, holds annual meeting and publishes a quarterly journal: *Journal of the American Psychoanalytic Association*.

AMERICAN ORTHOPSYCHIATRIC ASSOCIATION, 305 Lexington Avenue, New York 16, N.Y. A membership agency, holds annual meeting and publishes a quarterly journal: *American Journal of Orthopsychiatry: A Journal of Human Behavior*.

AMERICAN PSYCHOLOGICAL ASSOCIATION, 1515 Massachusetts Avenue, N.W., Washington 5, D.C. A membership and service agency, holds annual meeting and publishes *The American Psychologist,* the *Journal of Consulting Psychology,* and other publications.

AMERICAN ASSOCIATION OF PSYCHIATRIC SOCIAL WORKERS, 1860 Broadway, New York 23, N.Y. A membership and service agency. Publishes a quarterly journal: *Journal of Psychiatric Social Work.*

AMERICAN ASSOCIATION ON MENTAL DEFICIENCY, INC. Dr. Neil A. Dayton, Secretary-Treasurer (Superintendent of the Mansfield Training School, Mansfield Depot, Connecticut). A membership agency, holds annual meeting and publishes a quarterly journal: *American Journal of Mental Deficiency.*

NATIONAL ASSOCIATION FOR RETARDED CHILDREN. Mrs. Dorothy Moss, 565 Hale Avenue, Cincinnati, Ohio. An association of parent groups.

AMERICAN OCCUPATIONAL THERAPY ASSOCIATION, 33 West 42nd Street, New York 18, N.Y. A membership and service agency, holds annual meeting and publishes a journal: *American Journal of Occupational Therapy.*

MARRIAGE COUNSELING AND FAMILY RELATIONS

AMERICAN ASSOCIATION OF MARRIAGE COUNSELLORS, 370 Park Avenue, Suite 7E, New York 17, N.Y.

NATIONAL COUNCIL ON FAMILY RELATIONS, 5757 South Drexel Avenue, Chicago 37, Illinois. A service agency, publishes a monthly journal: *Marriage and Family Relations.*

SOURCES AND BIBLIOGRAPHY

Sources and Bibliography

Page 70, line 8, quotation from APPRAISING PERSONALITY by Dr. Mollie Harrower. Copyright 1952. W. W. Norton & Co., N.Y.

Page 101, line 16, quotation from FACTS AND THEORIES OF PSYCHO-ANALYSIS by Dr. Ives Hendrick. Copyright 1950. Alfred A. Knopf, Inc., N.Y.

Page 105, line 22, quotation from A GENERAL INTRODUCTION TO PSYCHOANALYSIS by Dr. Sigmund Freud. Copyright 1920–1935 by Edward L. Bernays. Liveright Publishing Corp., N.Y.

Page 119, line 21, quotation from PSYCHOANALYSIS AND GROUP BEHAVIOR by Saul Scheidlinger. Copyright 1952. W. W. Norton & Co., N.Y.

Page 140, line 18, quotation from PSYCHOANALYSIS: EVOLUTION AND DEVELOPMENT by Dr. Clara Thompson, in collaboration with Patrick Mullahy. Copyright 1950. Hermitage House, N.Y.

Page 153, line 12, quotation from INTRODUCTORY LECTURES ON PSYCHOANALYSIS by Dr. Sigmund Freud. Copyright 1929. George Allen and Unwin Ltd., London.

Page 196, line 23, quotation from "Evaluation of Electric Convulsion Therapy as Compared with Conservative Methods of Treatment in Depressive States" in The Journal of Mental Science (British Journal of Psychiatry). October, 1950.

Page 206, line 20, quotation from DIRECT ANALYSIS, The Collected Papers of Dr. John Rosen. Copyright 1953. Grune and Stratton, Inc., N.Y.

Page 210, line 19, quotation from PRESCRIPTION FOR REBELLION by Dr. Robert Lindner. Copyright 1952. Rinehart & Co., Inc., N.Y.

Page 221, line 25, quotation from IN SEARCH OF SELF by Dr. Arthur Jersild. Copyright 1952. Bureau of Publications, Teachers' College, Columbia University, N.Y.

INDEX

Index